PRAISE FOR "FINANCIALLY FREE IN 23"

"Highly recommended for anyone who doesn't understand the concept of money, how to use it for their best interest and comfort, and how to avoid living paycheck to paycheck."

KITTY LANE, AUTHOR

"[Financial freedom] is an expressed need in our society today that is addressed with amazing insights and powerful illustrations."

ANDY CLAPP, AUTHOR AND LITERARY AGENT

"If universities taught life skills, Hubbard's *Financially Free in 23 Weeks* would be the text and workbook of choice."

DR. MICHAEL J. SAVOIE, RYAN COLLEGE OF BUSINESS, UNIVERSITY OF NORTH TEXAS

"If you're serious about gaining control of your money instead of allowing your money to control you, *Financially Free in 23 Weeks* helps you understand your relationship with money."

CASEY SCHNEK, FAMILY AND TRAUMA THERAPIST

FINANCIALLY FREE IN 23 WEEKS

FINANCIALLY FREE IN 23 WEEKS

A COMMON "CENTS" BLUEPRINT FOR PEOPLE OF FAITH

ELIZABETH A. HUBBARD

PUNALUU DATA LLC

ISBN (print): 978-1-7358338-7-3

ISBN (ebook): 978-1-7358338-8-0

Cover Design by BookBrush

Photos, illustrations, and tables are owned by the author except where noted.

CONTENTS

PREFACE

The contents of this book have been successfully used by thousands of people throughout the country over the past twenty years. Over the years the principles contained herein – with the exception of those tied to an individual's religion – have been thoroughly vetted by the U.S. Department of Justice as meeting all of the requirements for financial education and credit counseling outlined in the laws and rules governing personal bankruptcy as administered by the Executive Office of the United States Trustee. The principles taught have also been vetted as meeting the requirements for financial literacy programs required by U.S. Department of Labor funding recipients. It is periodically updated to reflect the current state of the economy. This particular update adds a focus for people of faith.

I am not a licensed certified financial planner. Therefore, this book will not go into details of wealth management and financial investments governed by the Securities and Exchange Commission (SEC) or other governmental agency. Also, I am not a certified tax professional. While this book would not be complete without some discussion about retirement planning, long-term investments, and taxes, the information presented should be considered information, not advice. You should consult your own investment and tax professionals for advice.

This blueprint explores the role of faith in personal financial freedom, the psychology of money, your personal views about money, and the emotions associated with spending money. We will examine rising prices, declining services, and other economic changes making it increasingly difficult to get ahead financially. We will walk you through the process of learning the difference between needs and wants and how to prioritize them. You will be taught how to set and achieve goals. You will learn how to create a realistic earnings and spending plan based upon those goals. We'll also be showing you resources to help you stop losing ground and return to moving forward.

You will receive the greatest personal benefit when you use this blueprint in conjunction with the ***Financially Free in 23 Weeks Stewardship Workbook***. The workbook helps you apply the structural foundation and principles found in this blueprint.

Somehow, you got to where you are financially – it's really a relationship issue that very few understand. Unbeknownst to you, it probably started in your childhood. You saw how your parents, siblings, friends, and other associates earned and managed money. You saw how poverty, middle class, and wealth were portrayed on television, films, and even in video games. Whether you realize it or not, all of these contributed to your personal relationship with money.

It's easy to blame someone or something else. But, as you review some of God's will, and learn how others try to control your finances, you will learn that you are in control of your financial trajectory.

Financial freedom does not take place overnight. As guru Dave Ramsey puts it, it requires "baby steps." (By the way, Dave Ramsey, Robert Kiyosaki, and others of their ilk are great!) However, many people need to learn to crawl, then stand before they can start taking baby steps.

The five sections in this common "cents" blueprint are summarized in the following graphic.

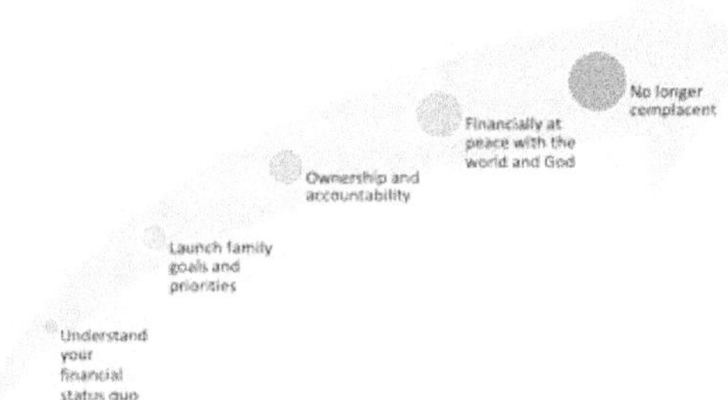

You probably didn't get to your current financial status quo overnight. Incorporating the changes you will need to make in your life often requires a bit of trial and error, but don't give up. Include your entire family and your God in your support system. Most people who use this blueprint start to feel financially free in about 23 weeks.

Real life examples will be presented. The cases presented are not meant to invoke judgment of any kind. They are designed to stimulate thought, create awareness, and encourage new habits. Take your time going through this book and the companion stewardship workbook so you can apply each of the principles over the next 23 weeks. It takes time and practice to be able to run with wealth building strategies.

SECTION 1 – UNDERSTANDING YOUR FINANCIAL STATUS QUO

"Dogs have no money. Isn't that amazing? They're broke their entire lives. But they get through. You know why dogs have no money? No Pockets." —
Jerry Seinfeld

Somehow, you got to where you are financially – but you're not ready to own it. It's too easy to blame someone or something else. You will probably encounter strong, strange feelings well up inside of you as you read and work through this section. As you review some of God's will, and learn how others try to control your finances, you will learn that you are in control of your financial trajectory.

Becoming financially free will not take place overnight. Allow yourself 5 weeks to complete Section 1. The ***Financially Free in 23 Weeks Stewardship Workbook*** is a weekly guide designed to help you apply the structural foundation and principles you're about to learn. The time you spend completing Section 1 is crucial to your ultimate success. Be honest with yourself. Embrace God's help.

WEEK 1
YES, IT IS POSSIBLE TO BECOME FINANCIALLY FREE

A deeply religious widow (whom we'll call Ms. Bessie), from one of the poorest counties in Louisiana, called me in tears. "Sheriff say I got to file bankruptcy. Court say I got to take your class first, but I ain't got no money. Sheriff say he got to sell my land next week 'less the court tell him I can stay." Once I got Ms. Bessie calmed down a bit, we discuss her precarious situation. Her husband's life insurance had paid off the mortgage on their mobile home and land, and had paid the property tax which was due at the time of his death.

When property tax bills were mailed out the following year, Ms. Bessie set it aside because she wasn't sure what to do with it. Her husband had always taken care of things like that. With the passage of time, she forgot about the bill. Another year rolled around, and another property tax bill arrived in the mail. It, too, sat neglected. The pattern repeated itself again. Unfortunately, not fully realizing the consequences of her decisions, she was now almost four years delinquent in paying her property taxes.

We examined the details of her income and expenditures. She drove an old car maintained by her auto-mechanic son. She worked at the local grocery store, where she was allowed to take home food items slated for disposal. "Cuttin' off 'em bad spots don't bother me none. All tastes the same in stew. 'Sides, sour milk make the best biscuits and chocolate cake ever!" The last time she bought a brand-new dress was for her husband's funeral. She lived very frugally – except for the money she paid in tithes and offerings. Almost 30% of her income was being given to her church. In addition to the 10% she paid in tithing, she was giving to the building fund, the youth ministry, the food pantry, and two missionary groups.

I explained to her that the government didn't care how much she gave to the church. They wanted their taxes. We had lengthy discussions about the principles of tithes and offerings as taught in the Bible as she struggled to reconcile her faith with the demands of the State. We then created a spending plan enabling her to pay the property taxes when due and still follow biblical teachings.

I juxtapose this humble widow to a family I counseled in Ft. Worth. They recently purchased a brand-new home on a two-acre lot. They drove a late model SUV and a late model truck. For play time, they owned a motorcycle, an ATV, and three dirt bikes. The husband had a good paying job, and they had a year's living expenses in the bank. They loved NASCAR, and frequently attended races at Texas Motor Speedway. Because the wife did not like to cook, they ate out at least twice a week. Their children participated in several extracurricular activities. Their parents lived in other states, so at least every quarter they paid for one of them to come out for a visit because they wanted their children to have a relationship with their grandparents. They were regular church goers, but did not pay any tithes or offerings. When asked why, the husband responded, "We can't afford to."

I was going to meet with this family at their minister's request. The minister explained, "We need a new roof and air conditioning system for our sanctuary. I'm asking everyone in our congregation to dig deep and pay a full tithe. What do you, as a financial educator, say to people who tell you they can't afford to pay tithing?"

"I usually don't say much of anything," I answered. "I guide them through a journey of self-discovery, taking a deep dive into all aspects of their personal money management, goals, and priorities."

The minister thought for a moment then said, "I've found that most people would rather talk about their worst sexual transgression than their money problems – even when money fights are destroying their marriages."

With a smile, I had to nod in agreement. Then, remembering the God-fearing widow in Louisiana, I said to the minister, "Jesus taught that where our treasures are, there will our heart be found."[1] This time, the minister nodded.

So, what and where are your treasures?

The economic stimulus packages and moratoriums issued as part of the federal government's response to the coronavirus pandemic created more financial bondage than any other governmental action since the New Deal. Don't get me wrong. There were people who genuinely needed help. While the intent was touted as benevolent and necessary to keep the economy from totally collapsing, it only delayed the inevitable. The time has come to pay the piper.

One consequence of governmental actions as part of the CARES Act, was millions of people suddenly found themselves with more money in their pocket from the government than they made working. I frequently heard, "Why work when the government will just give me money? Not only that, but the government won't allow my landlord to evict me if I don't pay the rent." (The government also did not allow foreclosures when mortgage payments became delinquent.) Therefore, in order to hire the employees needed to keep their businesses operating, employers were forced to increase compensation. Working has to be more lucrative than not working.

Another consequence was producers were not allowed to raise prices during the pandemic as they might otherwise have done. As a result, when certain ceilings were lifted, everyone started playing catch-up. If you're like me – and everyone else I know – inflation has really kicked you in the backside and has you dreading the momentary arrival of each new bill. For millions, 2022 and 2023 have been boom to bust years. Utilities, mortgage rates, transportation, and groceries continue double digit price increases.

I could show charts and graphs tracking the rate of inflation over the past couple of years, but you know as well as I do numbers published by the government are often a joke. They obviously don't purchase eggs, milk, bread and laundry detergent on a regular basis. Using myself as an example, the following table shows a few of the price increases I've dealt with at my local Walmart.

Item	June 2022	December 2022	% Increase
Dozen large brown eggs	$ 1.96	$ 4.23	116%
Gallon 2% milk	$ 3.44	$ 3.06	-12%
Sara Lee Bread	$ 2.98	$ 3.46	16%
Arm & Hammer Laundry Detergent	$ 8.87	$ 9.48	7%
Total	**$17.25**	**$20.23**	**17%**

I don't know about you, but my income did not increase 17% during that 6-month period. Did yours?

ARE *YOU* FINANCIALLY FREE?

If you worry about money, you are not financially free. When you worry, you tend to look at the worst "what-ifs" in life and become very pessimistic. Worry is an emotion – a useless emotion because it can keep you from moving forward, from gaining control over your life, and from reaching your goals. This can have a devastating impact on your life, especially if your current financial problems are putting a strain on your interpersonal relationships.

Are you struggling to make ends meet - *again*?

Have you ever wondered how you can afford to even live?

So how do we thrive – not just survive – inflationary times when the cost of everything is going up much faster than our income? We go back to the basics:

- Differentiating between "needs" and "wants"
- Creating a realistic spending and savings plan
- Implementing your plan
- Reviewing and adjusting the plan
- Repeating the above actions as life changes

The pandemic forever changed our lives. It changed the way millions of people make and spend money.

One of the biggest challenges many face today is the uncertainty of various debt forgiveness programs and moratoriums the federal government enacted. To you I say, pay your debts now and get it over with. It's going to cost you one way or another. Remember, a debt "forgiven" will ultimately be recovered through increased taxes, interest rates, costs of goods and services, etc. The moratoriums issued, such as the one for student loan payments, postponed payments. They did not always stop the accumulation of interest. They did not make the debt go away.

Nothing is ever truly *free*. This has been true since the beginning of man. Once Adam and Eve were cast out of the Garden of Eden, they had to toil by the sweat of their brows for their sustenance. Yet, we've grown accustomed to having a plethora of "freebies" – otherwise known as "benefits."

Another challenge facing consumers today is the recension of many "free" benefits. I recently received three email notices of *changes to benefits* for various services and accounts I have. One of them was from a MasterCard I use for online purchases. Probably like you, I usually just click my delete icon without bothering to pay attention to the change. I can't do anything about it anyway. Right? But because I've received so many notifications of changes recently, I decided to actually open the email and read what changes were taking place.

This particular MasterCard notified me that three of their benefits for card users, **purchase insurance, master rental waiver** and **world-wide automatic travel accident insurance, baggage delay insurance, and trip cancellation interrupted insurance** will no longer be available as of a certain date. No big deal, right? Not necessarily.

Now in and of itself this notification may not seem too bad because I haven't rented a vehicle recently nor have I done any traveling over the last year-and-a-half. But when I did travel a lot, I counted on these insurances in the event of an emergency. I actually used this benefit once when I went to conference in Orlando, Florida but my luggage went to Miami. The conference was over by the time my luggage caught up with me, so it was nice to have this small **baggage delay** insurance benefit to help cover the costs of the things I had to purchase in order to get through the conference.

The loss of the **purchase insurance** benefit is the one which really scares me. Probably like you, I've made increasing numbers of online purchases since the pandemic started. I used this particular MasterCard with the confidence that if there was ever a problem with a purchase, I would be able to get a refund and have the problem made whole.

So why are these seemingly *free benefits* no longer going to be available? The answer is because they never were free! The company providing the insurance protection to MasterCard for these benefits charges for them. The costs have increased so much since the pandemic started in early 2020 that it is no longer cost effective for this particular MasterCard to provide them to their customers without increasing fees, interest rate, or a combination.

I spent almost 20 years as a certified financial educator teaching financial literacy to people from all walks of life who were struggling to make ends meet. Some of my clients were paper millionaires without enough cash to make their debt payments. Some of my clients were doctors and dentists with tons of student loan and business debt while driving E-class Mercedes. Unfortunately, many of my clients were widows who had fallen prey to scammers. I have had clients who were generational welfare recipients yet somehow managed to obtain credit cards, or had been bilked by pay-day loan companies. I have counseled immigrants working hard for their American dream. I have sat with inmates filing for bankruptcy protection after paying court fees. However, the vast majority of those with whom I worked were people with good incomes, but whose spending habits were completely out of control. Most of them were under the impression they could become financially free simply by consolidating all of their debt or by filing bankruptcy. Unfortunately, the temporary relief felt was just that – temporary.

WHAT EXACTLY IS FINANCIAL FREEDOM?

Financial freedom means you are in control of your money. Your money is not in control of you. You choose when and how you are going to make your money. You also choose when and how you are going to spend your money. You do not care and are not overly influenced by what other people think about how you make or spend your money. Everything is legal. Everything is above board. You render unto Caesar that which is Caesar's, and you return to God a portion of all He has given you. Every decision you make with regards to money is made with deliberate conscious thought. You are not controlled by your emotions nor those of others. You are not mired in debt and hounded by debt collectors. You acknowledge work is good for the body and the soul. You teach your children how to work, how to save, and how to spend one wisely.

Financial freedom is a mindset. When you are financially free, you do not look down on others who may have less or more than you. You give thanks to God above for all the blessings He has bestowed upon you. As you move forward and upward you lift those around you. Those who struggle you help by teaching them how to fish.

When you are financially free greed has no place in your heart. Nor does envy. You do not covet what others have. You determine your own goals and priorities. You enjoy life. You acknowledge that at some point in time you will pass on and the only thing you will take with you is what is within your soul.

When you are financially free you do ***all*** you can to be self-reliant throughout your journey on earth. You understand the cost of convenience. Convenience has become a commonplace luxury for the recipients and a revenue generator for the provider. When you're financially free you are not a leach on society. You are a contributor to the greater good.

WHAT IS YOUR FINANCIAL STATUS QUO?

Think about your spending and savings habits. Have they changed much since the pandemic started? Are you better off now than you were before the pandemic?

The following tool will help you assess your personal style of handling money. Answer each statement by yourself. Then go through them again with your spouse or significant other. Are all of the answers the same? (Note: The *Financially Free in 23 Weeks Stewardship Workbook* contains all of the forms and other tools contained in this book. Digital resources can also be found at www.financiallyfreein23.net.)

FINANCIAL FREEDOM CHECK-UP

Review each statement to get a picture of your FINANCIAL STATUS QUO. Tally each item that is TRUE for you.

1. I have a written budget.
2. I set aside at least ten percent of my income for savings and investing.
3. I contribute the maximum amount to employer sponsored pension plans in order to get the maximum contribution from employers every year.
4. I avoid spending money to make myself feel better.
5. I make a list and plan all household and grocery spending in advance.
6. I follow a written budget.
7. My spouse/significant other and I pay our bills together.
8. I avoid using overdraft.
9. I avoid going into debt for entertainment purposes, including vacations.

10. I make no more than one trip a week to the grocery store.
11. I use manufacturer's and retailer's coupons when possible and send in for rebates.
12. I avoid paying fees and tips for local delivery services.
13. I avoid purchasing items I do not normally use just because I have a coupon for the item.
14. I look over sale flyers and comparison shop before I spend, especially for food and household items.
15. I comparison shop insurance policies when they come up for renewal.
16. I have enough liquid savings to pay all insurance deductibles when they occur.
17. I pay credit card purchases in full when the statement arrives and never pay interest charges or late fees.
18. I know how much I am paying for each subscription service used in my household.
19. I keep banking and shopping receipts, even for smaller purchases and record all of my expenditures.
20. I can always distinguish the difference between a "want" with a "need."
21. All members of my household help set our financial goals.
22. I only use my debit card when there is money in my checking account.
23. I have insurances to cover losses due to natural causes, accidents, and illness.
24. I regularly contribute to my house of worship.
25. I always consult my spouse before making purchases over $100.

Now add up the total number of TRUE items. Where do you stand?

- **22-25:** You are financially buff.
- **18-21:** You are right up there with the minority, but examine the statements that you did not tally. Each "True" statement brings you a step closer to financial freedom. How much

money could you save in 12 months if you answered "True" instead?

- **14-17:** Getting close, but no big payoff yet. Look at the statements you did not indicate as "True." If you want your assets to grow, look for saving in *every* area of your spending.
- **11-13:** You are at the halfway mark. However, if you do what you have always done, you will always get what you have now. If credit and debit cards are your bane, try something different – like hard CASH.
- **7-10:** Get off the money-merry-go-round! You are probably living from paycheck to paycheck. Poor spending practices may be doing you in. If you need a quick shot in the wallet, the average household spends 30 cents of every take home dollar on household and grocery items. You can make a big impact there the next time you go to the grocery store simply by making a list before you enter the store and only purchasing items on the list. When it comes to saving money, you must stop at nothing.
- **0-6:** What is that smell? Smoke from your credit and debit cards or payment apps being overused? Put your cards in a glass of water and freeze them solid. Uninstall your payment apps. If you aren't in credit counseling or bankruptcy court, both could be right around the corner. There's a lot to be said for using the old fashioned envelop system until you are in control of your money instead of your money controlling you.

Remember, each of your answers is very subjective. Most of you probably scored between 4 and 16. Becoming more aware of how, when, and why you spend money is an important step in becoming financially free.

If you kick a few bad habits, you can save a substantial amount of money in a short amount of time. For example, how much do you spend on coffee or lunch each day?

IT'S JUST A CUP OF COFFEE!!!

$4.95 x 1/week day = $4.95/day

$4.95 x 5 days/week = $24.75/week

$24.75 x 4 weeks/month = $99.00/month

$99.00/month x 12 months/year = $1,188.00/year

How much are **you** actually spending?

$_______ x _____ /day = $_______/day

$_______ x 5 days/week = $_______ /week

$_______ x 4 weeks/month = $_______/month

$_______ /month x 12 months/year = $_______ /year

As you continue through this book, you'll find that as your relationship with money changes, your interpersonal relationships will change, and your relationship with God will change. One client reported the greatest benefit his family received from going through the process contained in this blueprint was he and his wife no longer fought over money. When they had a difference of opinion regarding a financial matter, they'd ask themselves, "Are we exercising common cents?" Yes, they substituted the word "Cents" for "Sense." For them, it helped put things into perspective.

---

1. Paraphrased from Matthew 6:21, King James Version of the Holy Bible

THE ROLE OF FAITH IN FINANCIAL FREEDOM

"It is wise to work as well as study Torah; between the two, you will forget to sin." —Sayings of the Fathers 2:2

There are 3 basic tenets common to people of faith: tithes, preparing for future events, and stewardship of resources. In today's world, each of these usually involves money. Some people of faith don't think they can afford to participate in these tenets due to financial bondage. Shackles can be broken, but financial freedom doesn't take place overnight. It requires "baby steps." Often one needs to crawl, then stand before taking baby steps.

TITHES AND OFFERINGS

The earliest discussion of tithes and offerings I know of is found in Genesis 14 where Abraham gave tithes of all he possessed to Melchizedek. The Lord commanded Moses to have the children of Israel pay tithes. Perhaps the most famous passage of scripture regarding tithes and offerings is found in Malachi 3:8-11:

8. Will a man rob God? Yet ye have robbed me. But ye say, Wherein have we robbed thee? In tithes and offerings.
9. Ye *are* cursed with a curse: for ye have robbed me, *even* this whole nation.
10. Bring ye all the tithes into the storehouse, that there may be meat in mine house, and prove me now herewith, saith the Lord of hosts, if I will not open you the windows of heaven, and pour you out a blessing, that *there shall* not *be room* enough *to receive it.*
11. And I will rebuke the devourer for your sakes, and he shall not destroy the fruits of your ground; neither shall your vine cast her fruit before the time in the field, saith the Lord of hosts. [1]

The word *tithe* is the Hebrew word for tenth. Most Christian and Jewish denominations use the definition of tithes found in Old Testament. We acknowledge all things come from God, and we give a tenth of our increase back to Him. Pope Francis encouraged Christians to tithe cheerfully to God teaching that whatever they invest in the pursuit of Jesus will be returned a hundred times more. Rabbi Ethan Alder wrote, "The Talmud teaches that when one gives a tithe, he or she will eventually have more, not less. This "more" does not necessarily mean material gain; the simple joy of giving can and often does surpass the actual value of the sacrificed crops that made up the tithe." Other religions including Muslims, Sikhs, Hindus also have tenets of returning back to God a portion of what their Greater Almighty has given them.

As with all things in life, each person must choose for themselves whether or not they are going to pay tithes and offerings. I've heard many people of faith say they can't afford to pay tithing. If you are truly a person of faith, you can't afford not to. It is an act of worship. Some have even jokingly called tithing *fire insurance.* As you progress through the principles to financial freedom discussed in this book, you will discover how you really can afford to tithe.

Offerings are not so easily defined. Tithes and offerings are two different things. Offerings are **in addition** to tithes. Some sects preach the Law of Consecration under which members give everything to the church, then the church gives them what they need to sustain life. I am not talking about consecrating everything you have as an offering to the church.

Church offerings are usually requested for specific purposes. Offerings may be needed to make repairs to a place of worship. They may be needed to support missionaries. They may be used to help feed the poor, provide medicine, dig wells for clean water, and other humanitarian purposes. The amount one gives as an offering is individual.

PREPARATION

We all know we should prepare for unknown future natural and financial disasters. But knowing what we should do and actually doing it are often two different things. If you live in tornado or hurricane prone areas, you often have enough warning to pull a few emergency supplies together and move to a safer area. However, earthquakes come without warning as do chemical train derailments, tanker truck accidents, and a host of other disruptive things. While it is impossible to prepare for every future unknown, peace comes from knowing you have prepared the best you can to protect yourself and your family.

Think back to the beginning of the global shutdown due to the pandemic. How long were you able to survive on what you had stored in your home? What did you run out of first and how easily were you able to replace it? Think back to the last tornado, hurricane, blizzard, earthquake, fire, or other natural disaster which affected you. Was your grab-n-go survival bag fully stocked and ready to help you get through the next 72 hours?

In Chapter 41 of the Book of Genesis, we read the story of the Egyptian Pharaoh who had dreams of cattle and grain. These dreams troubled him because they were recurrent, so he sought among his people someone who could interpret the dreams. Joseph interpreted the Pharaoh's dreams as a message from God telling him there would be seven years of plenty, during which time he needed to prepare for seven years of famine. As events unfolded, the Pharaoh put Joseph in charge of gathering up grain from across the land and creating a vast storage program. When the predicted famine did arrive, not only were the people of Egypt able to survive, but people from other countries were able to obtain life-saving grain from Egypt as well.

Whether literal or allegorical, this God-given message is universal and has been throughout the history of man. There are cycles of good and bad times, and times of plenty as well as scarcity. Widespread catastrophic calamities such as hurricanes, drought, or the pandemic receive global media attention. Governments and relief agencies usually step in to help relieve the suffering and damage. This is not usually the case when individual famine strikes.

Individual famine can come in the form of loss of income, loss of shelter, loss of health, or loss of a loved one. Ideally, everyone – especially people of faith – will set aside some of the plenty in their lives for when famine strikes. We can't predict all the struggles and storms in life, not even the ones just around the next corner.

The parable of the ten virgins found in Matthew 25 is an example of Christ teaching His followers to prepare for future events. Occasionally this parable is used to urge people to prepare physically for the future. More often though, Jesus is talking about spiritual preparation.

When our lives turn in an unanticipated and undesirable direction, sometimes we experience stress and anxiety. One of the challenges of this mortal experience is to not allow the stresses and strains of life to get the better of us—to endure the varied seasons of life while remaining positive, even optimistic. Perhaps when difficulties and challenges strike, we should have these hopeful words of Robert Browning etched in our minds: "The best is yet to be" ("Rabbi Ben Ezra," in Charles W. Eliot, ed., *The Harvard Classics,* 50 vols. [1909–10], 42:1103)., but as persons of faith and hope, we know the best is yet to come.

In March of 1845 Henry David Thoreau decided to move out on the banks of Walden Pond and spend two years trying to figure out what life was all about. He settled on a piece of property owned by his good friend Ralph Waldo Emerson. He purchased an old shanty from a railroad worker, and tore it down. From the lumber from the shanty and the lumber from the woods, he constructed his own cabin. He kept meticulous financial records, and he concluded that for a home and freedom he spent a mere $28.12. He planted a garden, where he sowed peas, potatoes, corn, beans, and turnips to help sustain his simple life. He planted two and a half acres of beans with the intent of using the small profit to cover his needs. Small profit indeed: $8.71.

Thoreau lived quite independent of time. He had neither a clock nor a calendar in his little cabin. He spent his time writing and studying the beauties and wonder of nature that surrounded him, including local plants, birds, and animals. He did not live the life of a hermit—he visited the town of Concord most days, and he invited others to come into his cabin for enlightening conversations. When the two years ended, he left his cabin behind without regret. He considered the time he had spent there a proper amount of time to accomplish his purpose—to experience the spiritual benefits of a simplified lifestyle. He also felt he had other life experiences ahead of him. It was time to move on and explore other opportunities.

From his experiences at Walden Pond, Thoreau determined there were only four things a person really needed: food, clothing, shelter, and fuel. We'll be talking about food, clothing, and shelter in subsequent chapters. What I want to address in this chapter is *Thoreau's final necessity: fuel.* The fuel I want to discuss right now is both physical fuel and spiritual fuel.

Storing fuel in preparation for the future needs doesn't fit well within the financial planning categories contained in this blueprint. In fact, the entire subject of fuel is fraught with political overtones. Depending upon where you live, it may be extremely difficult to obtain, let alone store, fuel. You may have a wood burning fireplace and be able to obtain and store wood which you could use for warmth and possibly cooking should the need arise. You may have charcoal you can burn for heat and cooking. You may be able to purchase a back-up generator to power your home, but do you have the fuel or batteries the generator requires? You may be able to safely store kerosene or oil for lamps which will take care of your physical fuel requirements.

People of faith believe in a God – a supreme being. They believe they can communicate with God through prayer. They believe God will answer their prayers. They believe God can help them get through their daily trials and tribulations as well as major life-altering events. But this journey requires spiritual fuel.

Religious leader Elder L. Tom Perry talked about the five wise virgins, who had stored sufficient fuel to accompany the bridegroom when he came (see Matthew 25:6–10). "What is required to maintain a sufficient store of spiritual fuel? We must acquire knowledge of God's eternal plan and our role in it. We must be willing to humble ourselves and accept the fact that sometimes we need some divine help to weather the storms of life." As much as we think we are in total control of our lives, the only thing we really have total control over is how we prepare for and react to external forces be they man-made or natural. It helps to remember Ecclesiastes 3:[2]

1. To every *thing there is* a season, and a time to every purpose under the heaven:

2. A time to be born, and a time to die; a time to plant, and a time to pluck up *that which is* planted;

3. A time to kill, and a time to heal; a time to break down, and a time to build up;

4. A time to weep, and a time to laugh; a time to mourn, and a time to dance;

5. A time to cast away stones, and a time to gather stones together; a time to embrace, and a time to refrain from embracing;

6. A time to get, and a time to lose; a time to keep, and a time to cast away;

7. A time to rend, and a time to sew; a time to keep silence, and a time to speak;

8. A time to love, and a time to hate; a time of war, and a time of peace.

9. What profit hath he that worketh in that wherein he laboureth?

10. I have seen the travail, which God hath given to the sons of men to be exercised in it.

11. He hath made every *thing* beautiful in his time: also he hath set the world in their heart, so that no man can find out the work that God maketh from the beginning to the end.

STEWARDSHIP

Stewardship is the ethical responsibility man has to carefully manage all God has given him. Jesus taught this principle in the parable of the talents. The Lord expects us to both protect and increase the resources He provides for our use. In the case of money, not only do we need to use it wisely for the glory of God, but in the parable of the talents Jesus taught us to make it grow as well. Like the men to whom five talents and two talents were given, we need to report that we have used our several abilities and invested them wisely. We need to show how they increased. We should not be like the man who buried the one talent with which he was entrusted. Those who squander their money are considered slothful and unwise (Matthew 25:14-30).

Bishop Gérard Caussé spoke of the duty we have to honor and care for all of God's creations. Pastor Charles Bugg defines Christian stewardship as the responsibility for managing and utilizing intelligently the gifts God has given. A good steward is not only responsible for the financial blessings provided by God, but also the spiritual gifts given through the Holy Spirit.

The faith-based principles of preparing for hard times ahead, the regular payment of tithes and offerings, and being good stewards of gifts (think money) from God are hard to do financially, especially if you feel like you're just one paycheck away from bankruptcy. Know that you are not alone. Help is available both individually and in groups. You may be the perfect person to help someone else.

The Reverend Martin Luther King Jr., in his 1965 commencement address at Oberlin College, said: "All life is interrelated, and we are all caught in an inescapable network of mutuality, tied in a single garment of destiny. Whatever affects one directly, affects all indirectly. ... I can never be what I ought to be until you are what you ought to be. And you can never be what you ought to be until I am what I ought to be." In other words, no man is an island.

Today, preparedness, tithes, and offerings all involve money. Growing your money also has costs. Like the widow from Louisiana and the family from Ft. Worth, your own goals and priorities must be examined in order to find balance and peace. Each will be addressed in subsequent chapters. Your faith may be tested when you start looking at hard numbers. However, your faith may also be what empowers you. Regardless of the name by which you refer to divine power, don't be afraid to pray for help and guidance as you apply this blueprint to your life and become financially free.

----

1. King James Version
2. Ibid

WEEK 3
THE PSYCHOLOGY OF MONEY

"Tell me what you think about money, and I will tell you what you think about God, for these two are closely related. A man's heart is closer to his wallet than anything else." —Billy Graham

---

If the above quote from Reverend Billy Graham doesn't have you squirming a bit, I guarantee the next two chapters will arouse a myriad of emotions. Some may be quite strong – which can be good if you're open to self-reflection. Get curious. Seek God's guidance. Remember the Bible teaching that where your treasure is, there will your heart be also.

Many years ago, a neighbor of mine pounded on my door in a state of euphoria. Opening the door, she blurted, "We just bought a condo!"

I stepped away from the doorway as she twirled her way in and plopped down on the sofa. "You bought a condo?" I asked.

"Yep. We got high at a party last night and on our way home this morning we stopped at that new development going in near the office, and we bought a condo! You should see it! It isn't just boring straight boxy walls. Each room has unique angles and the windows allow you to have natural light all day long. We're paying a bit extra to have stained glass in the upper living room window." She was giddy with excitement.

I just looked at her like she was crazy. In my mind she was a little bit crazy. "So, when are you moving?"

"As soon as we can figure out how to pay for it."

I just stared at her for a moment. "Did you apply for a mortgage through the builder?"

"We gave them a check for $8,000 which was all we have in the bank right now. Now we have to come up with the rest of the money in the next 30 days. So, can you help us get a mortgage in the next 30 days?"

"Come back when you're not high," I said. "If you still want to go through with the purchase, I'll do what I can to help you find a good mortgage. If you don't want the condo, I can recommend a good real estate attorney."

Have you ever made a major purchase without paying attention to how you were going to pay for it? Have you ever felt "guilted" into making a purchase you would not have otherwise made? The most successful salespeople utilize psychology to their advantage.

Understanding the psychology of money is one of the best ways of gaining control of your finances and not letting your money control you. The psychology of money follows Maslow's five categories of human needs which dictate an individual's behavior.

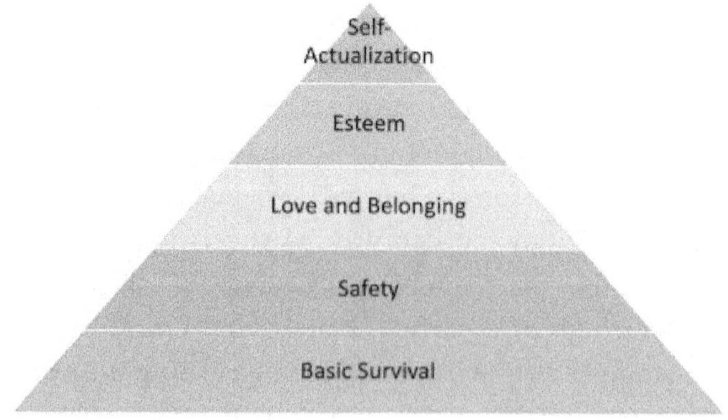

Maslow's Hierarchy of Human Needs

Basic survival needs are food, shelter, and clothing. In many situations, basic survival needs also includes transportation. But what really constitutes "basic survival"? Henry David Thoreau's conclusion included fuel.

Does your food intake consist of what you can grow yourself or do you dine in pricey restaurants? Are your clothes purchased from a thrift store or a chic boutique? I'm not saying you shouldn't have any in-fashion clothes, but do you really need to spend over $300 for a pair of torn, bleached out jeans when you could purchase a bottle of bleach and a pair of scissors for $5.00 and bleach and tear your old jeans? Would the people in the *in* clique really look close enough to know the difference?

Youth are especially bad about bullying or ostracizing peers whom they deem less than equals. School uniforms are a great equalizer. Some schools who do not require uniforms have determined that all students must carry the same backpacks and use the same tablets as a small step towards eliminating the distinction between the *haves* and the *have nots.*

Consumer marketers are experts in strategic marketing and product placement specifically designed to get you to spend money on items you may not need – and may not even really want. Women are their primary target, because women drive approximately 75% of consumer spending.

One subtle, but extremely effective, tactic consumer marketers use is the color palette. Women tend to pay attention to the colors used each year by the fashion industry. Other industries, such as home goods and publishing, follow suit. Simply changing the colors in an ad to reflect current fashion trends will catch a woman's eye.

Men are not as sensitive to marketing ploys targeting women. Male oriented consumer marketing focuses on size, weight, shine, strength, and sex. Men don't care about the color of a distributor cap, a chain saw, or a shop vac. They do care about horsepower and how pretty the receptionist at the gym is.

Consider the man who spends $3,000 on fancy rims for his truck. Do those rims make the truck run any better or smoother? Do the rims have cultural significance? Maslow knew that human emotions of love, belonging, and esteem are an integral part of basic human needs. For this man, spending money on fancy rims is his way of trying to belong to a particular group or be held in higher esteem by someone from whom he seeks approval. As just briefly illustrated, companies selling consumer products capitalize on those needs whenever possible. A former chairman of General Motors told an interviewer that the automotive industries are not selling transportation, they are selling emotion.

What impact do your emotions have on your purchasing decisions? Emotions are motivated by guilt, peer pressure, fear, depression, sadness, joy, pride, etc.

Marketers of consumer products spend millions of dollars playing on your emotions to get you to spend money on items you probably don't need. This is especially true during holidays such as Christmas, Valentine's Day, Mother's Day, and Halloween. Strategic marketing continually prompts you to shop earlier and earlier to catch the best bargains; to "show how much you care with..."; to do it "**NOW**"; and don't pass up that "priceless" moment.

The truth of the matter is, unless you have specifically budgeted for holiday spending, it is almost entirely driven by emotions. Did you know the average family spends over $200 every year on Valentine's Day and $800 on Halloween alone? The $180 you spent on a Mother's Day brunch may seem like a small price to pay to see your mother smile because all three of her children were with her at the same time – something which hadn't happened since you left home ten years ago. But if that $180 wasn't included in your spending plan, it had to come from somewhere. Is it now a debt?

People do not spend money just because they want or need a particular item. Advertising and marketing, done properly, helps people in their purchasing decisions. The goal of consumer advertising and marketing is to reach out to the consumer and tell them what they want and need before they know what they want and need. "Advertising is constantly bombarded by criticism. It is accused of encouraging materialism and consumption, of stereotyping, of causing us to purchase items for which we have no need, of taking advantage of children, of manipulating our behavior, using sex to sell, and generally contributing to the downfall of our social system" (Advertising Law & Ethics, Department of Advertising, University of Texas at Austin).

One of the most popular phrases used in advertising today is *BOGO* (Buy 1 Get 1 Free). Do you do the math when you see an ad which reads, "Buy 1, Get 1 Free"? If you only need a single item, could you obtain it at a lower price elsewhere? Do you read the fine print?

The art of strategic advertising is to make consumers, like you and me, think they are getting something for free or at a significant discount. Most of the time, if you stop to do the math, you will find you are actually spending more than you might otherwise spend had you not been influenced by the sign.

Strategic advertising is geared towards children as well as adults. Where are children exposed to advertising these days? On television, to some extent, but mainly on mobile devices. Parents may not even be aware of the embedded ads on apps for children.

What impact do your children have on your purchasing decisions – especially impulse shopping?

Retailers, especially grocery stores, deliberately lay out their stores so that the most frequently purchased items, such as milk and eggs, are at the back of the store. To get to the milk and eggs, you must walk down one of several aisles containing many other items which may or may not be needed. Baked goods, chips, and crackers are often seen on a table or other point-of-sale display right in front of the milk or eggs. These same baked goods, chips, and crackers can also be found in another place in the store specifically designated for baked goods, chips, and crackers. Why are these items also placed in front of the milk or eggs? It is called "Impulse Shopping." The store wants you to spontaneously put another item into your shopping cart which was not on your list of things you needed.

Melissa is spending the summer between her sophomore and junior year of college at home. She is working full time at Home Depot and part time at Cracker Barrel. Her goal is to save enough money so she can not only buy a car, but will not have to work during the school year as she has her first two years. Her parents are not charging her anything for rent or food. Melissa is earning $15/hour at Home Depot and $4.00/hour plus tips at Cracker Barrel. When she went to the bank to deposit her checks last week, she did not take any cash back because she had her tip money for gas and incidentals. Melissa's mom asked her to stop at the bakery after she went to the bank and buy fresh French bread for dinner. The bakery was next to a shoe store that had "the cutest summer shoes on sale." $800 later, Melissa arrived home with two new pairs of "the cutest shoes ever" and the French bread.

Can you relate to this example of "Impulse Shopping"?

UNDERSTANDING WHAT LED TO YOUR FINANCIAL DIFFICULTIES

"We were always going to be rich—next year." —Mark Twain

When I was growing up, whenever my dad got a raise at work, he always took the family out to a very nice restaurant as a celebration. He didn't take us anyplace local or casual. He took us to someplace really special with white table clothes, cloth napkins, fancy china, and snooty waiters – usually in San Francisco or Berkeley. We got to get dressed up in our Sunday best. Mom would get her hair done and put on her pearl necklace. We'd all be on our best behavior and practiced our best table manners. It would be a lovely evening. When we got home, we usually went straight to bed due to the lateness of the hour where we relived the sumptuous Chinese, French, German, Italian, or Scandinavian cuisine and ambiance in our dreams.

By the following evening, all of us kids were back in the dog-house because of all the money we were wasting when we left the lights on in empty rooms, or "accidently" dropped the liver and onions Mom had cooked for dinner. (Our dog, at least, enjoyed it.) Late at night when my parents thought we were all asleep, they would argue about how much money was being spent and how we needed to cut back. I knew what was coming next. The dreaded family council.

Family council was when we would all gather around the dining table and the new rules would be handed down. There was no discussion. It was a mandate. The grocery budget cut-backs were the worst! All of us, including Dad, had brown-bag lunches. All of us, including Dad, had to eat whatever Mom placed in front of us for dinner – even though it was burnt half the time. On Thursdays, whatever leftovers were in the refrigerator either went into a pot of soup or a casserole that Mom made up for dinner that night. Fridays were grocery shopping days, and the cycle repeated itself. We'd suffer through the budget friendly meals until the next celebration.

Luckily, one tradition that didn't change, was that birthdays were celebrations. The person with the birthday got to select the menu for all three meals – breakfast, lunch, and dinner. They also go to select their favorite desert. Other holidays were also gastronomical delights.

The contradiction of these huge pendulum swings was lost on me until I was married. My husband didn't understand why I frequently purchased very inexpensive cuts of meats neither of us liked, only to, (in his mind), splurge a few weeks later on a gourmet meal. Without realizing it, I had brought my parent's financial and budgeting practices into our marriage. The grocery budget was the arena in which it was most noticeable simply due to its daily presence in our lives.

The longer we were married, the more financial baggage was discovered. We both had made a lot of assumptions about the other's financial acumen. My husband was an accountant with several years of experience under his belt. We did not take time to sit down prior to marriage and find out if we were reading from the same book, let alone whether or not we were on the same page. As it turned out, we weren't even in the same library!

Case in point was the payment of tithes and offerings. We were both of the same faith, so I assumed we both had the same practices of paying tithes and offerings. We were having so many arguments about tithes and offerings that I finally said in a very un-Christlike tone, "Fine. I'll pay tithing on what I earn. What you do is between you and God."

Our financial difficulties stemmed from our individual systemic relationships with money (via our parents), our different interpretation of faith-based tithes and offerings, and our mutual stubbornness and insistence that we were right and the other person was wrong. It wasn't due to a cataclysmic disaster as is the case with many people. Our problems were emotional – psychological. We used money as a weapon. We used money to both reward and punish others. It took a divorce and a graduate degree to understand that I was the only person responsible for my financial difficulties.

Understanding what caused your financial difficulties may be an uncomfortable process. It may require deep introspection and unpleasant acknowledgements. For example, studies suggest men make impulse purchases and engage in emotional spending in areas which help them express their manhood, virility, and passions. Men tend to connect via activities, adventure, and excitement. Exhausted single parents are more likely to placate their child's temper tantrum with the acquisition *du jour* regardless of budgetary constraints. Divorced individuals, saddled with hefty family support payments, are unable to have the orders changed even if their employment status changes. Addictions usually put extra stain on finances.

Whether it is a single issue or multiple causes, you need to understand what led to your financial difficulties. It's equally important to identify which items you can control and which ones you cannot control.

If a picture is worth a thousand words, these photos say it all.

You're feeding your teenage son and his buddies. (Well, at least you know where they are!)

A freak hail storm sent golf ball and baseball size hail stones literally through three of your skylights. This same storm also turned the hood and top of your car into a moonscape.

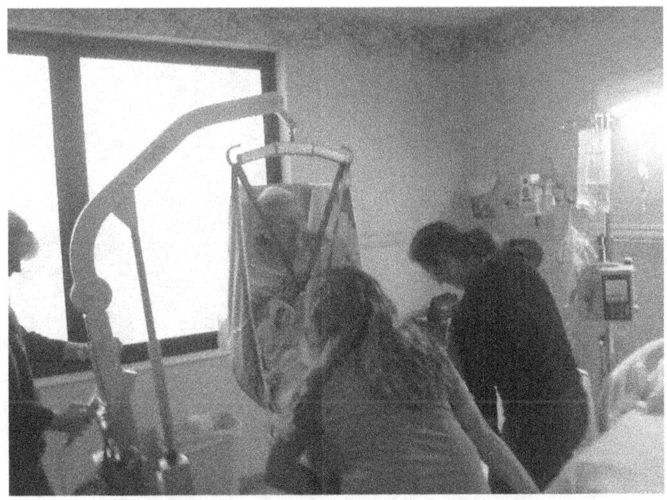

Hospital co-pays of 20% still came to over $40,000.

Furthering your education – at any age.

Frozen pipe burst flooding house, mold in walls, and subsequent flood remediation.

These pictures offer some extreme examples of things which might lead to financial difficulties. More often than not however, the root cause can be found in your relationship with money and the priories you've set for yourself and your family.

UNDERSTANDING NET WORTH VERSUS CASH FLOW

"Money will buy you everything but good sense." —*Jewish Proverb*

Do you know any broke millionaires? I do.

I counseled a thriving dentist who lived in an upscale neighborhood in Dallas, drove an expensive car, owned the building in which his dental practice operated, and sent his children to a posh private school. The problem was, he and his wife argued almost daily over the amount of money she was spending and how much was owed on their credit cards. They were barely covering the minimum payments. The problem was cash flow. The dentist received a salary from his practice every month. The amount, $35,000, should have been enough on which to live even after taxes and other withholdings, and tithing, but it wasn't because they were spending more than he brought home every month. His practice paid for their healthcare insurance. All they had to pay for was a small co-pay for prescription medications. He said they spent $1,200 a month on his mother-in-law's apartment since her husband died. Because they were not tracking expenditures, he had no idea where most of the money went. They did eat out a lot. They spent a lot for gas driving the children to and from school each day. They had professional lawn service and housekeeper. He enjoyed golfing and water skiing, so had a lot of big boy toys, paid green fees several times a month, (in addition to annual club membership fee), and storage fees for the boat, trailer, and jetskis. His wife loved shopping and decorating herself, the children, the house, and the office for every holiday and season.

"You're a paper millionaire," I told him. "Your monthly income is more than a lot of people earn in a year!"

"So why are we broke?" he asked.

With all of his high-priced education, neither he nor his wife fully understood the difference between net worth and cash flow.

Net worth is simple arithmetic. Add up all of your assets (what you own). Add up all of your liabilities (what you owe). Subtract your liabilities from your assets. That is your net worth. Using the dentist example above:

Cash in bank	$3,398
IRA	$225,136
Real Estate	$2,872,000
Vehicles	$49,500
Stocks & Bonds	$23,250
Boat	$10,000
Total Assets	**$3,183,284**
Credit Card debt	$57,856
Real Estate debt	$1,229,500
Vehicle debt	$47,000
Student Loan	$175,950
Boat	$15,975
Total Liabilities	**$1,526,281**
NET WORTH	**$1,657,003**

People often don't take into account the amount of money required to service their debt – especially for depreciating assets. It is not unusual for a person to owe more on their vehicle than it is worth. In this example, more is also owed on the boat than it is worth.

Cash flow is also simple arithmetic. Add up all of the money that comes in each month. Add up all of the money that goes out each month. Subtract the amount of money going out each month from the amount of money coming in each month. That is your cash flow. Based upon his guestimations our dentist's cash flow was:

Net Income (after withholdings)	$28,000
Tithing	$3,500
Mortgages (PITI)	$8,098
Mother-in-law's apartment	$1,200
Vehicle expenses	$3,700
Student loan	$459
Other debt payments	$4,000
Utilities	$672
Household groceries & stuff	$3,500
Private school expenses	$2,000
Recreation expenses	$1,000
Clothes and such	$1,750
Healthcare	$100
Monthly cash flow	**-$1,979**

This dentist and his wife were spending almost **$2,000 more** than he was bringing home each month. They did not have a spending plan.

It is important to have a positive net worth, but it is more important to have positive cash flow. When you have positive cash flow, more money is coming in than is being spent. In the case of this dentist, we had to start at the beginning reviewing each of the principles for financial freedom which meant adding his wife to the conversation and getting them on the same page.

SECTION 2 – LAUNCHING FAMILY GOALS AND PRIORITIES

"Someone stole all my credit cards, but I won't be reporting it. The thief spends less than my wife did." —Henny Youngman

Working together as a family, (regardless of size and age), you set clear, actionable goals upon which everyone agrees. You then prioritize those goals. You are learning to say "No" to influences that may pull you off course or distract from reaching your goals.

Allow yourself 4 weeks to complete Section 2. The ***Financially Free in 23 Weeks Stewardship Workbook*** is a weekly guide designed to help you apply the structural foundation and principles you're about to learn.

WEEK 6
KNOW BEFORE YOU OWE

"Money, if it does not bring you happiness, will at least help you be miserable in comfort." —Helen Gurley Brown

Most people have some kind of debt. Banks and other institutions have worked tirelessly since the 70's to have every person over the age of 18 indebted to them through the acquisition and prolific use of credit cards.

In the early days of credit cards, individual banks and stores created their own criteria for issuing credit cards, individually promoted their own cards, and individually processed the transactions that took place with their cards. Banks, wishing to increase revenue generated from the fees charged for credit card usage and also wishing to decrease the costs of promoting credit card usage and the costs of processing credit card transactions joined together and formed two separate associations. The primary purposes of these associations were to create brand awareness, consumer demand, and new market niches. These associations were named for their brands: Visa International and MasterCard International. These two associations changed the face of credit issuance and usage throughout the world.

Credit card companies such as Visa, MasterCard, American Express, etc., spend millions of dollars in advertisements to get you to use your credit cards. They are also working steadily to create new markets that will accept your credit card as payment for goods and services.

Under the Federal Truth in Lending Act, the cost of loans must be disclosed as both a finance charge (in this case the fee) and as an annual percentage rate (APR). These rules were more finely tuned under Federal Regulations passed in 2009, 2010, and 2011. By law every credit card statement must show how long it will take to repay the current statement balance, and the total amount you will pay, if you only make minimum payments. Most monthly minimum payments will cover the interest charged for that month, and a few dollars of the principal. Monthly minimum payments rarely cover additional fees imposed. Be G.O.O.D. to yourself, (Get Out Of Debt), and stay there. The long-term peace of mind will be more rewarding than the short-term pleasure that accompanies most debt.

It is very important that you read the terms and conditions card issuers provide with every new or existing debt account. Creditors are allowed to change terms and conditions at any time and for any reason.

Unplanned spending often results in unplanned debt. Virtually all debt has interest attached to it. The amount of interest charged is tied to the level of risk the creditor is taking when funds are loaned. If the creditor thinks there is a chance the money will not be repaid within the time agreed upon a higher interest rate will probably be charged. Lenders also have a variety of fees they charge borrowers.

In 1938, during the height of the Great Depression, J. Reuben Clark Jr. said, "Once in debt, interest is your companion every minute of the day and night; you cannot shun it or slip away from it; you cannot dismiss it; it yields neither to entreaties, demands, or orders; and whenever you get in its way or cross its course or fail to meet its demands, it crushes you." This statement is as true today as it was nearly a century ago.

By law, interest rates can **not** be buried in the fine print. Unfortunately, there are other costs that can be buried.

Read the Fine Print!!!

Read the Fine Print!!!

Most borrowers don't read all of the fine print – even though they sign attesting that they read it, and agree to all of the terms and conditions. Many lenders discourage the borrower from reading all of the fine print before signing because not only does it take time, it also warns some borrowers away from the transaction.

Companies are allowed to change their terms and conditions at any time provided they notify their customers of the pending changes. The following is an example of a recent notification by a cellular service provider.

"The majority of the changes are small things (like changing references to [company name] to "us", "we", and "our"; adding language to account for additional offerings (like Products and Wireless Internet); and updating phone numbers and website addresses). We're also rearranging the sections to group them in a way that flows better. We're adding additional information regarding our Privacy Notice, how we resolve disputes, and clarifying that you may still incur charges while an account or service is suspended. We're also making some additional disclaimers surrounding third party products and services and clarifying that the Agreement between us is not for the benefit of third parties."

Is there anything significant that jumps out at you? Were you aware ***"that you may still incur charges while an account or service is suspended"***? Reading the fine print will help you:

- Understand that interest compounds. That means that if the outstanding balance is not paid in full, the interest charged is added to the previous balance.
- Compare when interest starts accruing, and when the first loan payment is due.

- Understand all of the fees that are associated with the loan and which triggers activate them. Fees can sometimes equal or exceed the amount of interest actually paid.
- Understand how and when the lender communicates with a co-signer. If a co-signer is only notified that the borrower has missed one or more payments once the loan payment is 30 - 90 days late, the co-signer may struggle to bring the loan current.
- Learn about *deferral* or *forgiveness* clauses, the costs, conditions, etc.
- Know if a loan is classified as unsecured or secured debt.

Debts fall into three categories. The first category is unsecured debts. These are debts for which no collateral is required. Unsecured debts are sometimes called consumer debt. Examples of "Unsecured" debts are:

- Credit Cards
- Credit Cards in Collection
- Medical Bills (i.e. Dental, Doctor, Hospital)
- Non-card Accounts in Collections
- Signature Loan
- Student Loan (not government issued)
- Utility Loan

The second category is priority debts. Priority debts are governmental or court ordered debts which must be paid. Failure to pay priority debts can result in wage garnishment and asset seizure. Examples of "Priority" debts are:

- Alimony
- Child Support
- Restitution (in some cases)
- State Income Tax
- Federal Income Tax
- Government issued Student Loan

The third category is secured debts. These are debts for which collateral can be taken by the lender or creditor if the debt is not paid as agreed upon. Examples of "Secured" debts are:

- Mortgages
- Home Equity Loans
- Vehicle Loans (i.e. Auto, Truck, Motorcycle, Boat, etc.)
- Furniture & Appliance Loans
- Margin Accounts (Stocks & Bonds)
- Property Tax
- Mechanics Lien

A standard determinant used by banks and other lenders in assessing risk and thereby interest rates they will charge, is the individual's Debt-to-Income (DTI) ratio. This is determined by dividing total monthly debt payments by total net income.

Most lenders use the amount of debt shown on your credit report along with the monthly payment reported by the creditor when calculating your DTI. Consider the following example for a person whose net income (after taxes) is $5,162/month.

Creditor	Balance	Payment	DTI
SoFi	$19,548	$459	
BoA	6,351	298	
Capital One	8,121	241	
First United	35,432	673	
Total	**$69,452**	**$1,671**	**32.37**

In this example, 32.37% of this individual's monthly net income is required to make his current monthly debt payments.

Notice that interest rates are not included in this example. The reason is because variable interest rates are reflected in the monthly payment and the number of payments required to repay the balance owed in full.

When evaluating the amount of debt one has, simply looking at the amount that is owed is not sufficient. You must look at the real debt. Real debt is the amount you agree to repay each month times the number of remaining months.

Creditor	Current Balance	Current Payment	Remaining Payments	Total Real Debt
SoFi	$19,548	$459	48	$22,032
BoA	6,351	298	30	8,940
Capital One	8,121	241	39	9,399
First United	35,432	673	60	40,380
Total	**$69,452**	**$1,671**		**$80,751**

Lenders are required to disclose the total amount consumers will have to pay if they only make the minimum monthly payments. On revolving accounts, i.e. credit cards, a new calculation is included every month on your credit card statement. Unfortunately, few consumers pay attention to the disclosures.

In this example, if no additional debt is incurred, and I continue making only the current payment, it will take me two and a half years to pay off the BoA account, and five years before I am debt free. You will enter your own creditors, current balances, payment amounts, and remaining payments to calculate your real debt later in this book.

Debt consolidation loans are another type of heavily advertised consumer credit. Debt consolidation loans operate on the strategy of paying off all of one's short term debts, such as credit cards, with a loan for a larger amount, over a longer period of time, often with a lower interest rate than was being paid for the short term debt. The sales pitch is "put higher-rate debt behind you." This only works if the borrower does not take on any new high-rate debt.

People who are either maxed out on their credit card accounts or who do not have a Visa or MasterCard account are using payday loans for small loans. These loans go by a variety of names: "payday loans," "cash advance loans," "check advance loans," "post-dated check loans" or "delayed deposit check loans."

Fees for payday loans are not covered by the new Federal Regulations. These fees are typically a percentage of the face value of the check or a fee per $100 loaned. It is not uncommon to find "fees" ranging from

$10 to $18.62 per $100 borrowed. Some places charge as much as $25 per $100 borrowed. The following table shows the effective annual percentage rate (APR) a person who uses a payday loan will pay.

	Effective APR	
Fee/ $100	7-Day Payback	14-Day Payback
$ 5.00	521%	261%
$15.00	782%	391%
$18.00	938%	469%
$25.00	1,250%	625%
Note: The effective APR for active-duty military personnel is limited to 36%.		

The number of payday loan companies and locations are proliferating. One does not even have to meet face to face in order to obtain a small (up to $10,000) loan for a short period (usually one to two weeks) of time. The entire transaction can be handled online and the funds directly deposited. A "signature loan" is an example. These loans usually involve a credit check and sometimes use what is called a "lease buy-back." In this case, the firm initiates a sham purchase of the goods you claim you own, and purports to charge a fee to lease the goods, typically furniture, back to you. Here, the firm claims the furniture, not a post-dated check, is actually the collateral. The terms and schedule of payments are usually identical to those of payday loans.

A title loan (also called "auto title pawn") is a loan borrowed against the value of a motor vehicle. Title loans may be as high as $5000 or $15,000. The borrower keeps their motor vehicle and may drive it after receiving a title loan, but the lender keeps the title to the motor vehicle as security for repayment of the loan. The lender may also get a copy of the borrower's keys, much like a pawn shop. If the borrower does not make the payments on their loan, the lender will repossess their motor vehicle, sell it, and pocket whatever money he or she gets for it.

In conclusion, make sure you **KNOW** what a debt is going to cost you **BEFORE** you take it on. You are the only one who can determine if it is worth the cost.

DIFFERENTIATING BETWEEN NEEDS AND WANTS

"Money is a guarantee that we may have what we want in the future. Though we need nothing at the moment it insures the possibility of satisfying a new desire when it arises." —Aristotle

---

How do you decide how your money will be spent?

Do you have a plan or are all expenditures spontaneous?

Are you sometimes torn between spending money on things you really **want** versus things you **need**?

One of the biggest challenges you will face is differentiating ***needs*** and ***wants***. Even within the four basic survival needs previously discussed, the question must again be asked: "Is this a *need* or a *want*?" Take shelter as an example. Do you need a 2,000 square foot home or would a 1,500 square foot home satisfy your needs? Do you need a home which costs $325,000 or would a home with a $250,000 price tag satisfy your needs?

There is an old phrase, "house rich but cash poor." Do you use a credit card to purchase basic food, pay utility bills, or purchase basic transportation items (i.e., gas or bus pass) because you do not have sufficient funds in your bank account to pay cash for these items? (Use of a debit card is the same as using cash.)

Have you been charged overdraft fees during the past six months due to insufficient funds in your bank account to cover debit card and payment app transactions or checks written?

The answers to these questions can provide early warning signs of financial distress. When debt instruments, such as a credit card, are used to purchase basic needs because you do not have enough cash with which to purchase those items, you need to ask yourself a very difficult question each time you make **any** purchase: "Is this item I am purchasing a **need** or a **want**?"

The Reverend Billy Graham said, "Part of our problem with debt is that we have confused needs with wants. Yesterday's luxuries are today's necessities. We can possess nothing—no property and no person...It is God who owns everything, and we are but stewards of His property during the brief time we are on earth."

Put things into perspective by taking a few minutes to make a written list of your needs and wants. Include as many members of your family as possible in this activity. Allowing family members to provide input right from the beginning not only teaches them critical thinking, but enables them to become vested in the process of becoming financially free.

NEED	WANT
New car	3D gaming system
3-month emergency fund	Disneyworld vacation
School supplies	In-ground sprinkler system
Water heater	Rain gutters
Basketball shoes	NFL channels
Pay off credit card	Etc.
Etc.	

If you have debts, those should also be included in your spending plan priorities. Debts must be paid.

For people of faith, payment of tithes should be included in the *need* column. You will have to decide whether or not you include offerings in the *needs* column or you put it in the *want* column.

We also live under federal, state, and local governments that set laws which must be obeyed. For example, the law requires vehicle owners to carry insurance. If one owns a vehicle, insurance then becomes a *need*.

Immediately following the basic needs for survival mentioned above, is the need to provide safety and security. Adequate insurances are the easiest way of ensuring the safety and security of you and your family. Preparation for shortages of goods and food such as happened during the coronavirus pandemic shut downs is something people of faith would list as a need so they can provide for their family's safety and security. Reflect upon your own experiences when the shutdowns first occurred. Did you have enough food, toilet paper, and other household supplies in your pantry so you did not panic when you couldn't go to the grocery store 24/7/365?

Unexpected expenses have the potential to put you in a financial rut. Having cash on hand to cover day-to-day expenses and monthly bills is one thing, but how do you pay if the floor falls out from under you – literally?

In order to prepare for any unexpected expense, you need to build up an emergency fund of cash. In the case of home maintenance, a good rule of thumb is to set aside anywhere from 1% to 3% of your home's purchase price to cover improvements, upkeep, and repairs in a given calendar year. If the purchase price of your home was $250,000, you should have an emergency fund for home improvement and repair of $2,500 to $7,500.

While you're building up that cash reserve, home owners should consider including a few additional items in their list of needs. Maintaining your home on an on-going basis is a need. While money spent on small repairs will take away from your emergency fund in the short term, it'll also mean fewer surprises later. Plus, some things – like replacing a furnace filter – can be done without the help of a professional.

Monitor your home's systems, such as heating and cooling. Major appliances, plumbing fixtures, and your home's electricity also fall under this category. By keeping track of when old devices will likely need to be replaced, you'll experience less anxiety – and avoid the collateral damage you may face if they fail.

All families should have adequate medical insurance, and homeowner's or renter's insurance. If you have any motorized transportation, you should have vehicle insurance. Life insurance is important if your family is dependent upon your income to take care of their daily subsistence. Disability insurance and long-term care insurance become increasingly important as you age.

You are the only one who can define what the term "adequate insurance" means for your family. As you evaluate whether or not you have "adequate insurance" and have budgeted correctly for "adequate insurance", you should realistically access whether or not you have budgeted for and can easily pay all deductibles and items not covered by your insurance policies should the need ever arise. If you have a deductible of $1,000, you should keep $1,000 cash in a separate account so you don't have to go into debt to pay your deductible. When it comes to healthcare insurance, your deductible – or co-pay – could easily be thousands of dollars.

A minister spent a great deal of time counseling with members of his congregation who were having financial problems. His greatest challenge was getting people to recognize and accept the difference between necessities and wants. He said it was not uncommon for families not to have enough money for groceries but to be spending $160+ a month for television cable and streaming services and $340 a month for cellular telephones and service.

Contracts required by providers like cable or satellite television and wireless telephone companies have fees attached if the contract is not carried out to the end of the contract's term. These fees are usually tied to the cost of the equipment/hardware the consumer selected. However, some providers will lower monthly rates if you threaten to leave them for a less expensive provider or cancel service all together.

Advertisers and social pressure add to the difficulty in distinguishing between needs and wants. This is especially true with teenagers and young adults when it comes to their mobile device. Is a top-of-the-line smart phone with the latest camera functions a necessity?

This same minister said it was also not uncommon for families to turn to the church for assistance paying medical bills because they did not have adequate medical insurance nor sufficient savings to pay their deductibles and co-pays. The members requesting assistance often became belligerent when he told them to come back if they still couldn't pay all of their medical bills after selling their boats and ATVs.

What the members failed to remember is their minister had a stewardship over the church funds. Their minister had been entrusted with the church's resources and would be required to make a full accounting of how the church's funds were used.

Writing a list of needs and wants on a piece of paper requires thought. Thinking before spending may be a new experience for your family. Start with something everyone in your household can relate to – grocery shopping. The following form may help you get started. (The assumption is you created a menu for the week and you checked out the stores' weekly specials.)

Destination	Need	Want
Walmart	Milk Eggs Potatoes Baby carrots Light bulbs Toilet paper Bread Onion Ground beef Applesauce Chicken Rice-a-Roni Dog food	Potato chips Oreos Cinnamon rolls Pickles Gum Snack cakes Ice cream Popcorn
Target	Diapers Baby wipes Yogurt Laundry soap Lettuce Tomato	Soda Tortilla chips Salsa Guacamole Sleepers
Favorite Pizza		Extra-large supreme Wings

Very few people have so much money they can purchase what they want, when they want without regard to cost or other expenditures. Therefore, it helps to list your *needs* and *wants* in order of importance to you and/or your family. Yes this takes time, but your financial freedom is worth the effort.

Using our grocery store example, let's say that all of the *needs* are of equal importance, so we're leaving them as they are. Our wants are just that. They are items we want but don't need. Therefore, we have prioritized the items we *want*.

Destination	Need	Want
Walmart	Milk Eggs Potatoes Baby carrots Light bulbs Toilet paper Bread Onion Ground beef Applesauce Chicken Rice-a-Roni Dog food	Ice cream Pickles Oreos Cinnamon rolls Potato chips Gum Snack cakes Popcorn
Target	Diapers Baby wipes Yogurt Laundry soap Lettuce Tomato	Tortilla chips Salsa Guacamole Sleepers Soda
Favorite Pizza		Extra-large Supreme Wings

In this grocery shopping example, the items in the *needs* column get purchased first. With so much pricing data available online from retailers you should be able to know the cost of each item on your list before you enter the store. If you have enough money remaining in your food budget the items in the *wants* column can be purchased. If the cost of the *wants* listed exceeds your spending plan for the week, you have already prioritized them making it easier to decide what will be purchased.

Take this exercise to the next level by writing down a more generalized list of *needs* and *wants*.

NEED	WANT
Initial Brain Dump	
Water heater	Rain gutters
Pay car registration fee	Professional massage
Repair back fence	Mulch for garden
School supplies	3D gaming system
Pay off credit card	Disneyworld vacation
3-month emergency fund	NFL channels
Basketball shoes	In-ground sprinkler system
Replace brakes and tires on van	New window treatments
Well-puppy vaccinations	New car
Etc.	Etc.

Now prioritize your list of *needs* and *wants*. Remember, what is important to you may not be important to someone else. At a minimum there should be a consensus among the members of your household. Otherwise, this may be a source of contention.

NEED	WANT
Listed in order of priority	
Water heater	3D gaming system
Pay car registration fee	In-ground sprinkler system
Replace brakes and tires on van	Mulch for garden
Well-puppy vaccinations	Rain gutters
Basketball shoes	Professional massage
School supplies	NFL channels
3-month emergency fund	New car
Repair back fence	New window treatments
Pay off credit card	Disneyworld vacation
Etc.	Etc.

The process of prioritizing your needs and wants is time consuming. It requires open and honest communication among all participants – even if the participants consist of Me, Myself, and I. Internal battles are often the most difficult to resolve. The important thing to remember is that you are making conscious spending decisions.

It is not uncommon for you to say a *want* is more important to you than some of the *needs* you listed. There may even be some items you've included on the *needs* lists which you really don't care about – at least not right now.

Combined Prioritized List of NEEDS and WANTS
Water heater
3D gaming system
Pay car registration fee
Replace brakes and tires on van
Well-puppy vaccinations
Basketball shoes
School supplies
3-month emergency fund
In-ground sprinkler system
Mulch for garden
Repair back fence
Rain gutters
Professional massage
Professional massage
Pay off credit card
NFL channels
New car
New window treatments
Disneyworld vacation
Etc.

Yes, the back fence needs to be repaired, but until it falls over you don't consider it an urgent need. The water heater is another story. It is 20 years old and has started leaking. You may not mind letting the car registration slide as long as you aren't going anyplace where law enforcement may notice you're driving with expired plates. On the other hand, if a 3D gaming system will help keep your son and his buddies at your home instead of being out and about, the cost may be a small price to pay for your peace of mind.

As you repeat this exercise in all areas of your spending, you will be surprised at how much money you are actually spending on things you *want* but don't *need*.

Once you have prioritized your list of *needs* and *wants*, the next step is to analyze your list to determine whether or not there are acceptable alternatives and possibly lower costs to fulfilling/obtaining your *need* and/or *want*. This is especially advantageous when planning big ticket or emotional purchases.

This analytic process allows the family to assess and justify each *need* and *want*. Several questions should be asked and answered during the analytical process.

- How much will this need or want cost?
- What resources are available to achieve this need or want?
- What alternatives are there to this specific need or want?
- What would be the result to the individual/family if the need or want was eliminated?
- Can this need or want be accomplished more effectively and/or efficiently? This question may require creative thinking.

As you analyze your prioritized list of *needs* and *wants*, remember all of your analysis is based upon your own family's unique circumstances. What is right for you may not be right for someone else and vice versa.

ANALYSIS EXAMPLE 1

Need or Want: 3D Gaming System
Price of this need or want: $800

List the resources available to obtain this need or want:

- Salary
- Savings

Identify at least 3 alternatives to this specific need or want.

- Borrowing one from a friend
- Buy a less expensive system
- Go to a gaming entertainment center and use theirs

What would be the result to the family if this need or want is eliminated?

- It will be more difficult to know where my kids and their friends are and what they are doing.

Can this need or want be accomplished more effectively or efficiently?

- ?????

ANALYSIS EXAMPLE 2

Need or Want: New car

Price of this need or want: $38,000

List the resources available to obtain this need or want:

- $500 in the bank
- Weekly pay check

Identify at least 3 alternatives to this specific need or want.

- Buy a motorcycle
- Buy a cheaper car
- Repair existing car

What would be the result to the family if this need or want is eliminated?

- Job could be lost.

Can this need or want be accomplished more effectively and/or efficiently?

- Yes, by purchasing either a different vehicle or spending money to repair our current car.

ANALYSIS EXAMPLE 3

Need or Want: Have 3 months' worth of salary in liquid assets as an emergency fund

Price of this need or want: $18,000 in a savings account

List the resources available to obtain this need or want:

- Salary
- Sale of unused personal property

Identify at least 3 alternatives to this specific need or want.

- $10,000 in a savings account
- $5,000 in a savings account
- No savings. More credit cards with high debt limits

What would be the result to the family if this need or want is eliminated?

- Disaster in the event of an emergency

Can this need or want be accomplished more effectively and/or efficiently?

- Maybe.

- Get a second job
- Reduce spending in non-essential areas

WEEK 8
INSURANCE IS YOUR FRIEND

"A bank is a place that will lend you money if you can prove that you don't need it." —Bob Hope

---

Disclosure: *I am not now, nor have I ever been associated with the insurance industry. Everything in this section is information I use to educate myself and those whom I teach.*

Insurance is not cheap, which is the primary reason so many people in this country are under insured - **but neither is the cost of repairing lost or damaged bodies or property.** Consider Chris' story:

After being rushed to the Emergency Room by ambulance, Chris was admitted to the Intensive Care Unit (ICU) suffering from blood clots in his lungs and legs. After five (5) days in ICU, Chris was transferred to the acute care ward where doctors continued treating his blood clots in an effort to save his leg. Ten (10) days later, after the amputation of the lower part of his right leg, Chris was transferred to a rehabilitation hospital.

The bills for the ambulance, emergency room, ICU, acute care, surgeries, lab work, doctors and other attendants totaled $293,718. Chris will be in a rehabilitation hospital for at least a month at an estimated cost of another $200,000. The estimated cost does not include a prosthesis or ongoing physical therapy and medication.

Chris chose not to purchase any healthcare insurance claiming he could not afford it. However, he was able to afford the costs of recreational drugs for himself, sports leagues and camps for his four children, the latest in console gaming equipment, cell phones, tablets, and other electronics for himself, his wife, and their children, the care and feeding of 3 dogs, 2 cats, and 2 rabbits, and dinner menus featuring sushi, steak, and shrimp.

Health insurance is not the only insurance coverage Chris chose not to purchase. Chris does not have renter's insurance. Even though he lives outside of New Orleans, he is of the opinion that FEMA and his landlord will cover any losses his family may incur should another major hurricane hit New Orleans.

What exactly is insurance and what is adequate coverage? Insurance is a practice or arrangement by which a company or government agency provides a guarantee of compensation for specified loss, damage, illness, or death in return for payment of a premium. There 7 basic types of insurance. They are:

1. Life Insurance or Personal Insurance
2. Property Insurance
3. Marine Insurance
4. Fire Insurance
5. Liability Insurance
6. Guarantee Insurance
7. Social Insurance

Most insurances are elective, but some are required by law. An example is that in order to legally own an automobile in most states, you are required by law to have a policy for that state's minimum amount of automobile insurance.

In addition to those required by law, insurance policies should cover things which would cause you financial hardship if they are damaged or destroyed. It is a necessary and valuable financial service. After you take care of your basic needs of food, clothing, shelter and transportation, next consider your insurance needs. Insurance falls in the second tier of Maslow's hierarchy – Safety and Security. In your spending plans, ***insurance protection should come before*** investing or putting money in a retirement account.

The basic philosophy (economics) behind insurance is that a group of people will put a set amount of money into a pot for a specific purpose. Each pot will have its own set of rules governing who can contribute to the pot, how much must be contributed, and when the funds in the pot can be used. Let's use fire as an example. If a member of that group suffers a loss as a result of a fire, the loss will be fully or partially restored from the ***available*** funds in the pot. If multiple members of the group suffer a similar loss at the same time, there may not be enough available funds with which to pay out for all of the claims.

Before buying *any* insurance, be sure you understand what each type of insurance covers and what they do **not** cover. Purchasing insurance is extremely complicated because there are no standard baselines. Terms and definitions vary by company. Required coverage can vary by state.

HEALTH AND DISABILITY INSURANCE

The need for health insurance is not doubted by anyone in the United States today due to the high costs of medical care. Disability insurance is a secondary type of insurance related to health insurance that is desirable in certain self-employed situations and may be for other workers and career fields.

The general types of health insurance plans are:

- Group and/or individual health insurance for those up to 65 years old

- Medicare for those 65 and older
- Medicaid for the indigent and those in poverty

Within each of these types there are subtypes. Coverage and costs vary by provider, by state, and by county.

Health insurance typically pays a portion of *medical,* surgical, hospital, prescription drug and sometimes dental expenses and vision expenses incurred by the insured. *Health insurance* can reimburse the insured for expenses incurred from illness or injury, or pay the care provider directly. Individuals who do not have health insurance through their employer are supposed to obtain it through the "Marketplace" (https://www.healthcare.gov/). The "Individual Mandate" portion of the law currently is not being enforced on a federal level.

Each health insurance provider requires an application. Insurance providers are **NOT** required to approve an individual for the healthcare coverage or at the policy premium requested in the application. There are numerous factors each provider takes into consideration in determining what healthcare coverage they are willing to provide and at what cost. These include, but are not limited to:

- Gender
- Age
- Tobacco, Drug, and Alcohol Use
- Prior Medical Expenses
- Current Medical Conditions

The exceptions to this are active-duty service members and those age 65 + applying for basic Original Medicare.

Having healthcare insurance does not guarantee you will receive the medical care you want when you want it or where you want it. Each healthcare provider decides which insurance plans, if any, they will accept. Some providers choose to provide services only to those who pay cash.

The one exception is any hospital that has an emergency department AND accepts payments from Medicare is required to provide treatment to patients who need emergency medical services regardless of the patient's insurance status. The Emergency Medical and Treatment Labor Act (EMTLA) passed by Congress in 1986 explicitly forbids the denial of care to indigent or uninsured patients based on a lack of ability to pay. This law does not apply to ongoing care or preventative medicine.

Disability insurance is a secondary type of insurance related to health insurance. The purpose of disability insurance is to provide you with a portion of your prior/average salary to help pay for basic living expenses if you are unable to work for an extended period of time due to injury or illness.

There are 3 basic types of disability insurance:

- Short term
- Long term
- Permanent

Both short term and long term disability insurance are frequently offered by employers as part of their overall benefits package. Permanent disability is usually obtained through the Social Security Administration (www.ssa.gov). You should contact an insurance agent you trust to discuss disability insurances coverage and rates if you want to obtain disability insurance outside of your employer.

LIFE INSURANCE

If you were to die suddenly, what kind of financial hardship would result? Would there be dependents left without basic support? Would your burial costs impose undue hardship on others? These are important questions to ask and answer and possibly cover with life insurance policies.

LIABILITY INSURANCE

The most complicated insurance topic is liability insurance. You buy this to protect yourself from others. If your negligence or error should lead to damage of their property or, worse, their health, you should be prepared to cover these costs in case you are sued. Such liability coverage usually comes with your car and home or renter's insurance. So-called "umbrella policies" are also available for more general liability.

Coverage limits, in these cases, are usually based on your net worth and how much of it you can afford to lose? This is particularly important when establishing a long-term relationship, as well.

RENTER'S INSURANCE

Most renter's insurance policies do cover wind damage, but some companies in coastal areas affected by hurricanes exclude this from standard coverage. One policy may cover wind damage caused by hurricanes, and another may require you to purchase an additional rider or renter's hurricane insurance.

In states where a natural disaster has been declared by the president, the uninsured or under-insured *might* receive federal aid, but it is capped at just over $30,000. A typical payment is likely to be much less. For more information about renter's insurance, see https://www.trustedchoice.com/renters-insurance/coverage-types/catastrophe-renters.

Back to our example of Chris. Chris applied for Medicaid. He thought he would automatically be approved since he had not been working for the past year. Chris thought all of his medical related expenses would be 100% covered. Because Chris lived in a community property state and his wife worked and had been supporting the family solely on her earnings, Chris' application for Medicaid was denied.

Whether it's FEMA, Medicaid, Social Security Insurance, or unemployment insurance, don't assume you will automatically qualify. Like non-governmental policies, contributions are expected and there are rules governing who is eligible to receive funds, when, how much, and for how long.

If you don't know exactly what you're doing, get a second opinion from someone other than the insurance agent or salesman. Consult others who know and understand these types of insurance.

Insurance policies and the people selling them appeal to your fears.

The same coverage may be in both your basic life, disability, and auto policies. If you've set these up to cover what you can't afford to lose, you definitely need to do it again as your circumstances change. What you can afford to lose if you have young children at home is likely very different from what you can afford to lose if there are no children at home.

Many insurance companies will give you a great deal on premiums if you buy multiple policies from them (life, health and auto). Ask for multiple policy discounts and compare quotes of several companies. Before you buy any insurance coverage make sure you shop around and compare prices. Rates may vary widely between insurance agents and companies. Start by asking the following questions and analyzing the answers:

Q: How much car insurance do I need?
A: There are specific state insurance requirements. Your insurance agent will know what is required in your state. You may want more than the minimum insurance required. Talk with your agent about what is appropriate for you in your area and what the additional coverage will cost.

Q: Do I need Auto Gap insurance?
A: The difference between the actual fair market value of your auto, which is usually what insurance will pay if it "totaled" and the loan amount you owe on the car may be substantially different. You may need insurance to cover this difference if you are "upside down" or "underwater" on the car.

Q: How much insurance coverage should I buy for my house?
A: In selecting an appropriate amount of coverage, be sure to avoid the most common consumer mistake - insuring your home for what it costs to sell (the market value), rather than what it costs to replace. Homeowner policies are designed to cover the cost of reconstructing your home should it ever be destroyed. Therefore, you should select an amount of insurance that represents the replacement value of your home. Look for a company who will assist you in the valuation of your

home. Additionally, look for a company that provides a payment basis called "extended replacement cost." This payment basis helps you rebuild your home even if it exceeds the amount of insurance on your policy.

Q: I rent. Do I need insurance?
A: If all your clothes, the appliances you own, your TV, stereo, jewelry and computer were destroyed in a fire, could you replace them, immediately, out of pocket without going into debt? If you said "No", you need renter's insurance. You may be surprised to learn that renter's insurance is not very expensive. The only thing you're insuring is the contents of your apartment or house. It's certainly cheaper than replacing all your possessions after a disaster. Renter's insurance provides the security of knowing that if you lost everything today, you wouldn't be forced to start from scratch. Renter's insurance can even cover you for personal possessions which are not in your residence at the time of the loss – for example, stolen luggage while on a vacation. You can't count on your landlord's policy to cover your possessions.

Creating a table or matrix showing the type and amount of coverage you seek can help you compare the various policies available. Just a word of warning, though. Stand firm with each company with whom you speak. You need to be able to ask each company identical questions – questions important to you – and receive answers to those questions. Otherwise, you will not be able to do a true apples-to-apples comparison.

	Company A	Company B	Company C
Premium for $10,000 uninsured motorist			
Premium for $5,000 per passenger medical			
Premium for $1,000,000 collision liability			
Etc.			

If you shop for insurance online, never give out personal information like name, address, telephone, and especially, Social Security number. If you do, insurance agents may call or contact you. If you provide your Social Security number, you can expect a check of your credit. The rates you can expect to pay for insurance are determined by a number of factors including your credit report. (Multiple inquiries on your credit history can hurt your credit rating. You risk identity theft when you give out your Social Security number.) Information-only quotes based on age, sex, health, and medical information, or car and home details, are available on some company websites without asking you to identify yourself.

Check out the company before you purchase a policy. Lower premiums may sound great for your budget, but if the company doesn't pay well for claims, this can be worse. Each state has a list of registered insurance companies licensed to operate in that state. States also maintain lists of complaints consumers have filed against insurance companies.

Whether or not you should use an insurance agent is a matter of personal preference. Most insurance agents earn commissions only. Some, such as those who work for USAA, are salaried. With Internet resources at your disposal, you can educate yourself to avoid shady sales practices and select an agent or company who offers real value.

Term life insurance is cheap and simple enough for most people to make an educated purchase, start to finish, on the internet or by phone from a direct insurance provider. On the other hand, long-term care insurance is about as complicated, and expensive as it gets. Even after extensive online research, many people will still benefit from the services of an independent financial planner, particularly one with experience in long-term care issues.

Auto, home, renter's, and disability insurance fall in the middle. They aren't as complicated, but they are much more likely to lead to a claim than age-limited life insurance. When it comes to making a property claim, an effective local agent can be worth their weight in gold. Also, with liability and medical claims, procedures can be very tricky and decisions are rarely clear-cut. A proactive agent can be an invaluable guide. Of course, it always depends on the agent, the circumstances, and to some extent, the way the company handles claims.

In addition to the traditional insurance agent, there are a few other options. An independent insurance agent represents a number of insurance companies and may more objectively weigh pluses and minuses across many companies and types of insurance.

A good licensed financial planner can build insurance into your overall financial plan, should you or your situation call for a professional. The key here, again, is independence. Work with a fee-only financial planner. Many insurance salespeople may represent themselves as financial planners and try to help you with financial and insurance decisions.

A good agent should help you with an annual insurance review. As your life situation changes, so do your insurance needs. Probably the simplest example is life insurance. The bottom line is most people need less life insurance every year as they build savings and approach retirement. On the other side of the coin, most people don't need any life insurance until the baby arrives. You might want to drop collision and comprehensive insurance when your car is paid off and you have the equivalent of the fair market value in a savings account.

SETTING AND REACHING YOUR GOALS

"Money is the best deodorant." —Elizabeth Taylor

Did you deliberately plan to be where you are financially at this point in your life? How's it working for you? You won't become financially free overnight. You need to plan how you are going to achieve freedom.

Financial planner Tom Corley spent five years observing more than 350 "rich" and "poor" people, how they live, work and even sleep, and captured them all in his book, *Rich Habits: The Daily Success Habits of Wealthy Individuals*. He defined "wealthy" as earning at least $160,000 annually and holding at least $3.2 million in assets. Corley defined "poor" as income under $30,000 a year and less than $5,000 in assets. Corley found:

- 81% of wealthy maintain a to-do list vs. 19% for poor.
- 80% of wealthy are focused on accomplishing some single goal. Only 12% of the poor do this.
- 67% of wealthy write down their goals vs. 17% for poor

- 88% of wealthy read 30 minutes or more each day for education or career reasons vs 2% for poor.
- 86% of wealthy believe in life-long educational self-improvement vs. 5% for poor.
- 23% of wealthy gamble. 52% of poor people gamble. (This includes lottery tickets.)
- 79% of wealthy network 5 hours or more each month vs. 16% for poor.
- 70% of wealthy parents make their children volunteer 10 hours or more a month vs. 3% for poor.

Take an honest assessment of your habits. Those with rich habits thrive. Those with poor habits survive – just barely.

Creating and accomplishing goals is a wealthy habit. Goals are specific, measurable tasks or activities in which you, (individual/family), will engage. There is no limit to the number of goals you may or should set. There should be a combination of both long-term and short-term goals. Goals should address both needs and wants. Ideally, each goal will have two or three alternative ways of achieving it.

You should create goals just like businesses do. Schedule a time for everyone in the family to meet together in a setting not subject to interruptions. Devices should all be turned off. Explain to children that you are going to ask them to think of something they would like to have, do, or be. This will be a "goal" for them to achieve. Explain how goals usually do not happen immediately. It is something they will have to work towards.

No goal is too insignificant not only because it is important to someone, but because most goals have a price tag attached. Goals can be for one or more individuals or for the entire family.

It is important for all members of the family provide input into the setting of goals. It is even more important that each member of the family agrees to help meet the family's goals especially when the goals are used to determine how money will be spent.

Identifying, prioritizing, and analyzing needs and wants was discussed in Chapter 5. You can enhance that process in this step by asking another difficult question before any purchase, "How does this purchase support our goals?"

DEVELOPING YOUR GOALS

What do you want to accomplish, do, or be?

When do you want to mark it as "done"?

These are the first two steps in developing your goals. The "what" and the "when" need to be as specific as possible. For example, your goal may be to publish a book by the end of this calendar year.

This goal meets the "what" and the "when", but is so broad you could easily feel overwhelmed. To make life easier on yourself, it is best if you break the goal down into more manageable segments: In order to publish a book by the end of this calendar year, you are going to write one chapter every week starting this week and continuing for the next x number of weeks, i.e. 15.

These sub-goals may still be too broad. You may want to break down the goals to another level. For example, you may say, I am going to spend one hour a day writing. Alternately, you may say, I am going to spend every Sunday from 1 – 6pm writing.

Further development of your goal to publish a book by the end of this calendar year requires putting all of the sub-goals together in a timeline to make sure you haven't missed any mission critical tasks. Here is an example assuming you're going start pursuing your goal in February.

FEB	MAR	APR	MAY	JUN	JUL	AUG	SEP	OCT	NOV	DEC
Write Chps. 1 - 4	Write Chps. 5 - 9	Write Chps. 10 - 14	Write Chps. 15 - 20	Send to editor revise as needed	Cover Design Finalize book format	Obtain Editorial & book reviews from 10 sources	Publisher Approval	Finalize Ads Detail Launch plans	Pre-Publish Marketing	Publish And Launch

Using visuals such as a timeline can help you determine whether or not you have set a realistically achievable goal.

Next, list what you *need* and *want* to help you reach of your goals. Alternative ways of achieving each goal should also be written down.

Also, needs and wants should contain a description of how it will help you reach your goals. Other than that, no judgments should be made at this point.

Self-interest motivates both buyers and sellers in a society based upon capitalism such as the United States. This self-interest, or selfishness, will become evident very quickly as each member of the family contributes to the lists. Using the family's goals that have been agreed to as a benchmark for identifying needs and wants will help redirect individual selfishness towards the welfare of the family.

FEB	MAR	APR	MAY	JUN	JUL	AUG	SEP	OCT	NOV	DEC
Write Chps. 1 - 4	Write Chps. 5 - 9	Write Chps. 10 - 14	Write Chps. 15 - 20	Send to editor revise as needed	Cover Design Finalize book format	Obtain Editorial & book reviews from 10 sources	Publisher Approval	Finalize Ads Detail Launch plans	Pre-Publish Market-ing	Publish And Launch
NEEDS AND WANTS										
<ul><li>Quiet working area (N)</li><li>Good lighting (N)</li><li>Back-up power supply (N)</li><li>Good speech to text software (W)</li><li>Auto back-up to cloud (N)</li><li>Book writing and formatting software i.e. Vellum (W)</li><li>Etc.</li></ul>				Repeat the process of listing all of your needs and wants for each of your sub-goals and goal-setting periods. Make sure to label each item as a "need" (N) or a "want" (W).						

Repeat the process of listing all of your needs and wants for each of your sub-goals and goal-setting periods. Make sure to label each item as a "need" (N) or a "want" (W).

ANALYSIS OF EACH NEED AND WANT

Let's continue in our example of publishing a book by the end of this calendar year. You've listed your *needs* and *wants*. Now you're going to analyze each of them which includes identifying alternative options.

FEB	MAR	APR	MAY	JUN	JUL	AUG	SEP	OCT	NOV	DEC
Write Chps. 1 - 4	Write Chps. 5 - 9	Write Chps. 10 - 14	Write Chps. 15 - 20	Send to editor revise as needed	Cover Design Finalize book format	Obtain Editorial & book reviews from 10 sources	Publisher Approval	Finalize Ads Detail Launch plans	Pre-Publish Market-ing	Publish And Launch
NEEDS AND WANTS										

• Quiet working area (N) • Good lighting (N) • Back-up power supply (N) • Good speech to text software (W) • Auto back-up to cloud (N) • Book writing and formatting software i.e. Vellum (W) • Etc.	Repeat the process of listing all of your needs and wants for each of your sub-goals and goal-setting periods. Make sure to label each item as a "need" (N) or a "want" (W).

ANALYSIS OF NEEDS AND WANTS	
• <u>Quiet working area (N)</u> *send kids to bed; turn garage or shed into work area; train dog not to allow anyone to come into the bedroom; work after hours at the office; go to the library; sit in the car* • <u>Good lighting (N)</u> *buy a desk lamp, buy a filtered large display screen* • <u>Back-up power supply (N)</u> *buy extra laptop batteries* • <u>Good speech to text software</u> (W); *make do with current speech to text software; learn to type faster;* • <u>Auto back-up to cloud (N)</u> *buy an additional external hard drive with auto save;* • <u>Book writing and formatting software i.e. Vellum (W)</u> *continue using Word; hire someone else to do the formatting* • Etc.	Repeat the process of analyzing all of your needs and wants for each of your sub-goals and goal-setting periods. Make sure to label each item as a "need" (N) or a "want" (W). Think of alternatives – regardless of how bizarre they may seem.

Repeat the process of analyzing all of your needs and wants for each of your sub-goals and goal-setting periods. Make sure to label each item as a "need" (N) or a "want" (W). Think of alternatives – regardless of how bizarre they may seem.

RANKING OF NEEDS AND WANTS

Continuing in our example of publishing a book by the end of this calendar year, you've analyzed your "needs" and "wants." Now you're going to prioritize each of them.

RANKING OF NEEDS AND WANTS	
<ul><li>Quiet working area (N) *send kids to bed; turn garage or shed into work area; train dog not to allow anyone to come into the bedroom; work after hours at the office; go to the library; sit in the car*</li><li>Good lighting (N) *buy a desk lamp; buy a filtered large display screen*</li><li>Auto back-up to cloud (N) *buy an additional external hard drive with auto save;*</li><li>Good speech to text software (W); *make do with current speech to text software; learn to type faster;*</li><li>Back-up power supply (N) *buy extra laptop batteries*</li><li>Book writing and formatting software i.e. Vellum (W) *continue using Word; hire someone else to do the formatting*</li><li>Etc.</li></ul>	Repeat the process of ranking all of your needs and wants for each of your sub-goals and goal-setting periods. You are the only one who can truly determine priorities. You might want to highlight details requiring specific resources.

Goal-based budgeting is not a fast nor is it an easy process. It is, however, necessary if you are going to make life-changing habits to become financially free. This process can work for anyone, regardless education, income, or age. It does require a very high level of commitment and discipline. Don't forget to pray for help as you work to become financially free.

The following is a simple form to help you start your financial freedom journey. Start with 2 or 3 easily achievable short-term goals. Add a picture to help you and others understand the objective. It will take practice, but the more goals you set and reach, the less frustrated and discouraged you and your family will be.

Simple Goal Planning Worksheet as of February 1st			
Goal	Completion Date	Minimum Needs	Estimated Cost
Basic 72-Hr Survival Kit 1 per person Use old backpack or gym bag to hold items	Feb. 14th	3 liters water 9 granola/protein bars 3 jerky sticks 3 fruit sticks/snacks Hard candy Chewing gum Disposable wipes 3-days prescription/OTC meds Small soap Dental floss Flashlight Batteries Basic First Aid Kit Pocketknife 3 Solar Blankets Waterproof Matches Change of underwear Extra Socks, hat, gloves Waterproof poncho Small Radio Pencil/Pen Paper/note pad	$30/kit
Pay tithing each paycheck	Feb. 9th Feb. 26th	Commitment Determination	$97 $97
Food Pantry Service	Feb. 28th	2-3 hours	0

SECTION 3 – OWNERSHIP AND ACCOUNTABILITY

"Intaxication: Euphoria at getting a refund from the IRS, which lasts until you realize it was your money to start with." —From a Washington Post word contest

Because everyone in the family had input in the creation of goals and agreed to the priorities, fights about money have ceased. Each member of the family is accountable for their financial actions.

Allow yourself 7 weeks to complete Section 3. The ***Financially Free in 23 Weeks Stewardship Workbook*** is a weekly guide designed to help you apply the structural foundation and principles you're about to learn.

CREATING YOUR SPENDING PLAN

"Money often costs too much." —Ralph Waldo Emerson

It has been said that if we fail to plan, we plan to fail. Preparing for the future is as important as preparing for today. Preparing for today may be as simple as setting the alarm clock to help you get to work on time. Preparing for the future may be purchasing a funeral and burial plan. Both involve planning for things important to you and your family. There are times when even the best planning you do may not be sufficient for the challenges you will face. Perhaps the hardest thing for anyone to do is to plan for the unexpected which may occur sometime in the future. Unfortunately, if there is one thing the past few years have taught us, it is that no one is immune from catastrophic national or global economic events. The difference between how well each person weathers the storm is contingent upon how prepared they were for it.

When creating a spending plan, you need to include everything for which you spend money. This includes all junk food, fast food, haircuts, manicures, utilities, vehicle maintenance, gas, meal services, streaming apps, internet, cable TV, cell phone, gym and any other payment contracts or subscriptions into which you have entered, extracurricular activities, etc. For people of faith, your spending plan should include tithes and offerings. It should also include building up your storehouse for future times of need.

Preparing a budget is nothing more than a way of organizing your income and expenditures. Think of it as your spending plan. One way of organizing your money is to say you're going to spend a certain percentage each on needs, wants, and savings. As we previously discussed, this works for some, but doesn't take your goals and priorities into account.

There are four types of expenses in a budget: fixed monthly, variable monthly, periodic, and discretionary.

Fixed expenses are expenses in which the amounts are the same every month. A mortgage payment (or rent), vehicle payment, and child support are examples of fixed expenses.

Variable expenses are expenditures which generally occur every month, but the actual amount of the expense varies. Food and utilities are examples of fixed expenses.

Periodic expenses are expenditures which do not occur every month but will occur sometime. Vehicle registration is an example of a periodic expense. Medical expenses and vehicle maintenance are expenses which may occur any time that also fall within the periodic expense category.

Discretionary expenses are wants. They are not essential for sustaining life or for obtaining and maintaining employment.

Within each of these four types of expenses are *needs* – expenditures you must make, and *wants* – expenditures that you would like to make. Generally, discretionary expenses are only things you *want* but don't *need*.

You control the amount you spend on variable expenses. But even the so-called "fixed" expenses are not completely fixed. For example, your house payment may not change from month to month, but you may refinance your mortgage to get a lower payment or purchase a less expensive house. Your landlord may raise your rent, but you could move into a cheaper place. Your car payment may be the same every month, but you can always trade in your car for one with a lower payment. Your cell phone bill may be the same every month, but you could select a different plan with a lower monthly payment.

One of the major differences between fixed and variable expenses is how quickly you can lower the expenses to suit your needs. Keep this difference between fixed and variable expenses in mind as we review your spending plan later, and think about ways you can reduce your spending in the future.

You have set goals for yourself and family. You have listed your needs and wants. You have analyzed your needs and wants by determining whether or not they help you obtain goals. You have considered alternative means for obtaining your needs and wants. You have determined the impact the elimination of the need or want would have on you and your family. Finally, you ranked your needs and wants in order of priority.

It has not been easy accomplishing these tasks. Some may think it is time wasted. Others may simply be glad that part is over and you can move on. Fortunately, or unfortunately, depending upon your point of view, the analysis of your needs and wants and the goals to which they are tied, is an on-going process.

Forget everything you have spent or are currently spending when you prepare your spending plan. Do not think the budget will be limited by the amount of income available. Based upon the priorities set and alternatives considered, resources may be expanded beyond current income. (Refer to the Chapter 16 for weird but great income streams.) This part of the process may require several revisions to resource allocation. For example, you may have allocated 32% to housing as number 1 need priority. If your resources total $3,000.00, 32% equals $960.00. Is that amount for rent/mortgage only? Did you include utilities (water, electricity, gas, sewage, etc.) in your list of needs or in your determination of how much to allocate to housing?

Since home mortgages have been used as an example, remember that Home Equity Loans and Home Equity Lines of Credit are also mortgages (second, third, etc.) against your property and must be accounted for accordingly.

The one exception to the earlier statement of not considering anything you currently spend in the budgeting process is debt payments. The minimum debt payments must be included in the resource allocation and budget unless the debt is being retired as part of the planning process that has gone on so far. For example, the decision may have been made to sell the Corvette and purchase a Taurus. The proceeds from the sale of the Corvette would pay for the Taurus and eliminate the remaining 18 payments on the Corvette. If that transaction takes place immediately, there is no need to include the Corvette payments in the budget. Therefore, if your current minimum debt payments total $528.52 per month and your resources or income total $3,000.00 per month, the minimum allocation should be 17.6%.

There are three types of debt, which will be discussed in detail in a later session. For planning purposes at this juncture, you may want to separate debt associated with housing and transportation from all other debt. A home mortgage is a debt. A car loan is a debt. Both may be acceptable based upon the goals that have been set and the priorities given to home ownership and vehicle ownership. However, in the event the debts for a home and/or car consume an inordinate percentage of the available resources, there may be a need to reassess the percentage to be allocated from this point on. Let's say you are paying $1,039.86 each month for mortgage, insurance, and taxes out of your available $3,000.00. That equals 34.7% of your available resources. Is this an acceptable percentage? Where does home ownership fall in your list of priorities? Is there enough left of the total amount designated to needs to meet the other needs listed? Is there a way of reducing costs without sacrificing the goal?

INCOME IDENTIFICATION

"Too many people spend money they haven't earned, to buy things they don't want, to impress people they don't like." —Will Smith

What resources do you have? For most people, their resources are their income and their assets. Money invested in stocks and bonds is an asset which could be turned into cash to use for a need or want. A boat is an asset which could be sold if you wanted something else more than you wanted the boat. Your house and car are assets and thus resources.

In creating your spending plan, you will first review your net income or take-home pay. We do this in 3 steps.

1. Review all of the gross incomes you have already listed.
2. Review all of the deductions you have listed. One of the reasons many people do not fully understand the differences between gross and net income is with direct deposits, many people do not look at their statement which details deductions.

3. Examine your net income from all sources. The amount available after deductions is your net income or take home pay. This is the amount of money against which you will create your monthly budget.

If your income varies significantly from one month to the next, you will need to repeat this process on a monthly basis.

Some of these items, such as tax preparation, vehicle maintenance and licenses & registration occur periodically. I recommend you "budget" 1/12th of your annual expenditures for these items in your monthly budget. If you put these budgeted amounts into a separate savings account, you will have the necessary funds when they are needed without going into debt.

As you start entering your income, make sure you think of all types of income you receive. People often receive money they don't consider income such as unemployment insurance, child support, or disability insurance. You should list all types of money (income) you receive on which you rely to pay rent, purchase groceries, care for children, etc.

Enter the **gross** amount (before deductions) received or earned from each "Income Type." Remember, there is no limit to the number of entries you may make for each "Income Type."

Income Category Detail	Per Pay Period	Monthly Total
Salary		
Salary		
Retirement, Pension		
Social Security, Disability		
Child Support		
Unemployment		
Investment, Passive		
Side Hustle		
Other		
Total		

(**NOTE:** All of the forms in this book are found in the *Financially Free in 23 Weeks Stewardship Workbook.* They can also be downloaded at www.financiallyfreein23.net. The formulas are in the background and will automatically total all of your columns for you.)

TAXES AND OTHER REQUIRED PAYROLL DEDUCTIONS

"Money is like manure. You have to spread it around or it smells." —J. Paul Getty

Do you understand why and when money is deducted from your earnings? You may be one of the millions of people who do not realize that funds can be withheld from social security income, investment income, and other income sources for a variety of reasons, the most common of which are State and Federal income taxes and medical insurance. If you do not have access to an itemization of your deductions, contact your Payroll Department and obtain a copy as you will need the information to complete this section.

Don't fall into the trap of thinking a deduction cannot be changed or eliminated. Some think getting a large tax refund each year is a way of having extra money for vacations, home repairs, or other items they want. Many people mistakenly think money automatically deducted and being put into a savings or retirement plan of some sort (i.e. 401K), or stock options is good financial planning. However, if they are thousands of dollars in debt and are paying higher interest rates on their debt than they are earning on their savings they may be better off eliminating optional deductions until their debts are paid. Insurance is important, but it needs to be the right kind and the correct amount for your current needs.

If you are self-employed, make sure you include self-employment tax in your list of deductions. These funds need to be put into a separate account as they must be sent to the IRS by certain deadlines.

Payroll Deductions Category Detail	Per Pay Period	Monthly Total
Federal Withholding Tax		
FICA/Social Security		
Medicare		
State Withholding Tax		
Local Withholding Tax		
Unemployment Insurance		
Union Dues		
401K/Retirement		
Medical Insurance		
Dental Insurance		
Vision Insurance		
Life Insurance		
Other Employer Offered Insurance		
Wage Garnishment		
Other		
Total		

(**NOTE:** All of the forms in this book are found in the *Financially Free in 23 Weeks Stewardship Workbook.* They can also be downloaded at <u>www.-financiallyfreein23.net</u>. The formulas are in the background and will automatically total all of your columns for you.)

WEEK 13
DEBT: MONEY YOU OWE

"Compound interest is the 8th wonder of the world. He who understands it, earns it - he who doesn't, pays it!" —Albert Einstein

---

"If you do not actually receive cash, but receive goods or services in advance of cash, is that really a debt?" This question, asked by a college student, underscores the need for a concise definition of "debt" as used in this blueprint. **A debt is an obligation to pay. A debt is an obligation to pay for goods and services received without full payment. A debt is an obligation to repay money which was borrowed. A debt is an obligation to pay taxes, assessments, and orders issued by a governmental agency or court.**

Most creditors, those who loan you money or provide goods or services in advance of full payment, fall into three main categories. The first are the unsecured creditors. These are debts for which no collateral is required. Unsecured debts are sometimes called consumer debt. Examples of "Unsecured" creditors are:

- Financial Institutions or Companies who issue Credit Cards
- Dentists, Doctors, Hospitals, etc. when the bill is not paid in full
- Financial Institutions, Companies, or individuals who issue Signature Loans
- Financial Institutions who issue Student Loans
- Loans or unpaid bills from Utility Companies

The second category is secured creditors. These are debts for which collateral can be taken by the lender or creditor if the debt is not paid as agreed upon. Examples of "Secured" creditors are:

- Financial Institution, Company, or Individual who issues Mortgages
- Financial Institution, Company, or Individual who issues Vehicle Loans (i.e. Auto, Truck, Motorcycle, Boat, etc.)
- Financial Institution, Company, or Individual who issues Furniture, Electronics & Appliance Loans
- Financial Institution, Company, or Individual who issues Margin Accounts (Stocks & Bonds)
- A Contractor who works on your home and files a Mechanics Lien

The third category is priority creditors. These are debts ordered by governmental agencies for which collateral can be taken by the lender or creditor if the debt is not paid as agreed upon. Examples of "Priority" creditors are:

- A court order to pay child support
- A Governmental Agency authorized to collect Taxes
- A Judgment (In some states a judgment becomes a lien against personal property and/or wages and bank accounts.)
- A government issued student loan

I could cite a lot of current laws, rules, and regulations, but they can be confusing. Suffice it to say, avoid this type of debt at all cost. If you truly feel as though you have no other option for a truly urgent need, consult with your spiritual advisor, your rabi, priest, or minister. They may help you find options not previously considered.

As you enter the information requested about each of your debts, do not worry about whether they are secured, priority, or unsecured. Be as accurate as possible. Use good faith estimates when the actual amounts are unknown. (**NOTE:** All of the forms in this book are found in the *Financially Free in 23 Weeks Stewardship Workbook.* They can also be downloaded at www.financiallyfreein23.net. The formulas are in the background.

Creditor	Type	Amount Owed	Interest Rate	Payment (A)	Remaining Payments (B)	Total Interest	Real Debt (A x B)

As you work towards financial freedom, you'll realize you **can** pay off all of your debts. Some experts recommend paying off the debt with the highest interest rate first. However, my clients found that paying off the debt with the smallest outstanding balance first provides a huge mental win. It goes back to the opening premise – you have to learn how to crawl first.

Whether you call it debt rollup or debt snowball, the process is the same. List all of your debt by the outstanding balance, smallest to largest. Pay off the debt with the smallest balance first. Do what you can to find a few extra dollars each month to pay the remaining balance. Once that debt is gone, add the amount you had been paying on the first debt to the next smallest debt. When the second debt is paid off, you take that sum and add it to the third debt on your list. As you make each final payment on a debt, you're going to feel elated. The world is going to look brighter. You're going to feel more self-confident. You're going to believe you will shake off the bonds of debt. You can be financially free.

CONSCIOUS SPENDING

"If you think nobody cares if you're alive, try missing a couple of car payments." —Earl Wilson

---

For years there has been a 50/30/20 rule of thumb for budgeting recommendations. Fifty percent of your net income should go towards **needs**, 30% for **wants**, and 20% for **savings**. That is a great generalized rule of thumb, but as previously discussed, the goals you and your family have set for yourselves along with religious practices of paying tithes and offerings will impact this rule. A more realistic guideline for people of faith is 60/20/20.

Monthly living expenses are often listed in the following very general categories:

- Housing
- Utilities
- Necessities
- Transportation

- Insurance (Not taken out of payroll)
- Education
- Healthcare
- Savings & Investments
- Unsecured & Priority Debts
- Household Goods
- Pets/Animals
- Entertainment
- Gifts & Donations
- Miscellaneous & Other

The problem with general budget categories such as these is that it is too easy to forget some of the details which should be included. This blueprint will guide you through the details within each category so you capture everything you need to create a realistic spending plan.

If you are one of the millions of people who have lost some of all of their income in the past few years, you may have used credit cards to pay for some of the expenses associated with searching for a new job. You may have also used credit cards to pay some or all of your living expenses. Either way, you have seen your debt load mount and cash reserves dwindle.

Most people do not realize how much it costs to search for new or better employment and therefore fail to include those expenses in their spending plan (aka budget). Some of the items that need to be included are:

- Cost of transportation to job interviews, which may include parking, tolls, airfare, lodging, etc.
- Cost of cell phone, email, and fax for immediate contact by potential employer
- Cost of personal grooming as trimmed hair, clean well pressed clothes, and polished shoes are critical for a good first impression
- Cost of resume preparation and follow-up/thank you notes
- Cost of personal business cards for networking

Another area in which people make unplanned expenditures is for non-profit organizations. A "small" purchase here and another "small" purchase there for the benefit of your non-profit may be detrimental to you even though it is benefiting the entity. Would you pay $8.00 for a small box of thin minty cookies inside a grocery store? Why then do you spend $8.00 for a box of Girl Scout Thin Mints being sold at outside the EXIT door? And let's get real about this, isn't it more like $25 you end up spending because a single box of Thin Mints won't even make it home with you. If you know you're not going to be able to resist the Thin Mints, include it in your spending plan as part of Gifts and Donations. Check with your tax professional, but only a small part of that $8.00 box of cookies is really the cost of the cookies. The rest is part of the organization's fundraising campaign and therefore tax deductible.

Even though it may be hard to tell the Senior Citizen's Club you will not be able to provide the materials for the ladies' quilting day because you need the $40 to pay your gas bill, you need to take care of your own family first. Getting out of debt and staying out of debt is part of taking care of your own family.

Most financial gurus will tell you to pay yourself first, but if you are a person of faith, you should pay God first. Then pay yourself. We will use these priorities in this blueprint. (**NOTE:** All of the forms in this book are found in the *Financially Free in 23 Weeks Stewardship Workbook*. They can also be downloaded at www.financiallyfreein23.net. The formulas are in the background and will automatically total all of your columns for you.)

RELIGIOUS CONTRIBUTIONS

Donations to the church made by people of faith may consume more than 10% of your net income. By the time you add everything up, you may find you are donating closer to 12 - 13% of your total net income. Keep a careful record of all of your donations as they may be tax deductible. Your tax professional can provide you with specifics.

Religious Donations Category Detail	Per Pay Period	Monthly Total
Tithes		
Offerings		
Other		
TOTAL		

SAVINGS & INVESTMENTS

After you have paid God, pay yourself – even if you're starting with only a few dollars a pay period. If you are participating in a company sponsored 401K or other retirement plan, that counts as paying yourself first.

Savings and investments fall into two main categories: short term or liquid savings and long term or managed. Ideally, everyone should have at least $1,000 of emergency cash. This may be in a financial institution, a home safe, or under your mattress. A thousand dollars may not earn any interest, but it goes a long way towards giving you peace of mind when you suddenly have to purchase a new tire or end up at an out-of-network 24/7 Urgent Care clinic. After you have your emergency cash stashed away, each household should build up liquid savings of at least 3 months' essential living expenses with the goal of having 6 months' all-inclusive living expenses set aside. Essential living expenses would be the sum of non-discretionary housing and utilities, transportation, debt payments, grocery (food, soap, diapers, etc.), insurance, and work-related items you've included in your spending plan. These savings will allow you to absorb large, unexpected expenses without taking on more debt. If you become unemployed, underemployed or lose time from work due to injury or family needs, your savings can help you meet basic needs when your income is temporarily reduced or eliminated.

We recommend allocating 15% of your net income for savings and/or investments. Even when your budget seems impossibly tight, there are ways to make room for savings if you are willing to make difficult choices. Think of how free you will feel knowing you have a safety net in place.

As mentioned previously, most long-term investments are managed funds governed by state and federal regulations. We recommend you consult a licensed professional financial advisor to discuss the myriad of options available to you.

Savings & Investment Category Detail	Per Pay Period	Monthly Total
Annuities		
Retirement, IRA, etc.		
General Savings Account		
Certificate of Deposit		
Stocks & Bonds		
Digital Currency		
Other		
TOTAL		

Even if you can't budget for savings right now, you can start a rainy-day fund by setting aside your loose change every day. Hold a garage sale and add your earnings to the fund. Cash in small rebate checks and throw them into the pot, too. The amounts are so small they won't affect your monthly budget, but the savings add up quicker than you might think.

Check in with your financial planner and/or tax professional on a regular basis. As with everything the government influences, rules keep changing. For example, Secure 2.0 made 4 key changes to Roth IRA retirement plans:

1. **Catch-up contributions for high earners**: If you're age 50 or older and have maxed out your 401(k) contributions for the

year, you will now be able to contribute an additional $7,500 in catch-up contributions.

2. **SIMPLE and SEP IRAs**: These plans, which are common among small businesses, can now be designated as Roth IRAs.
3. **Employer match for 401(k) plans**: Employers can now give employees with 401(k) plans the choice to have their contributions matched on either a pre-tax or after-tax basis.
4. **Distribution rules**: Starting next year, Roth 401(k)s will no longer be subject to minimum distribution rules, meaning you won't be required to take money from them if you don't want to.

Protect your investments by keeping up with the governing rules.

HOUSING

Housing expenses include all of the following:

- Mortgages or rent
- Homeowners or renters' insurance
- Property tax
- Homeowner's Association Dues
- Home maintenance, including landscaping
- Security deposits

If your housing expenses are greater than or equal to the recommendation of 25% of your net income, you should consider reducing them. Some suggestions are:

- If you are renting, consider moving to a less expensive residence.
- Check your homeowners or renters' insurance policy. Are you paying for coverage you don't need? Could you make the deductible higher?

- Make sure you are taking advantage of all possible property tax exemptions.

Do you have more house than you need? Would downsizing reduce all of your housing expenses?

Housing Category Detail	Per Pay Period	Monthly Total
First Mortgage or Rent		
Second Mortgage		
Third Mortgage		
Homeowner's or Renter's Insurance		
Property Tax		
Homeowner's Association Dues		
Security Deposit		
Yard Maintenance		
Home Maintenance		
Other		
TOTAL		

UTILITIES

Utilities include all of the following:

- Home heating oil
- Electricity
- Gas
- Water
- Sewer

- Garbage
- Telephone (land line and cell phone)

If your utility expenses are greater than or equal to the recommendation of 7%, you should consider some of the following suggestions:

- Try to use less air conditioning and home heating
- Consider different providers who may offer lower costs
- If you have both a land line and a cell phone, consider eliminating one of them

Cable/satellite and internet expenses are not included in the list of utilities because they are included in other categories which cover more discretionary expenditures.

Utilities Category Detail	Per Pay Period	Monthly Total
Electricity		
Gas		
Propane		
Septic, Sewer		
Water		
Garbage, Trash Collection		
Basic Cell Phone, Land Line		
Security Deposits		
Other		
TOTAL		

FOOD, HOUSEHOLD ITEMS, CLOTHING, & OTHER NECESSITIES

Your food, household supplies, and other necessary expenses should not exceed 10% of your monthly net income. Food is one of the biggest budget busters in a family's spending plan. Diligent meal planning complete with a detailed shopping list is the first step to being able to stick to your plan. Purchasing only those items on your shopping list is the next step.

Food, Household Items, Clothing, & Other Necessities Category Detail	Per Pay Period	Monthly Total
Food & Household Supplies		
School/Work Lunch		
Diapers/Formula		
Clothing		
Work/School Uniforms		
Babysitting/Childcare		
Other		
TOTAL		

If you still need to cut back spending in this category, consider making school and work lunches at home before leaving for the day. The average work lunch of a meat sandwich, chips, pickle spear, and drink costs $14.00 – assuming you pick it up yourself. Delivery fees and tips can easily add another $7 for a total lunch tab of $21.00. The same lunch made at home and brought to work costs $6.00 - $8.00.

Use coupons, purchase in-store brands rather than national brands, and shop at stores with lower prices. Make items at home from scratch rather than purchasing pre-prepared foods. For example, most people can save about $2.50 each time they purchase a muffin, if they made muffins at home then kept them stored in the freezer until they wanted one. Making lasagna at home from scratch for a family of 4 is about $9.00 cheaper than purchasing pre-made packaged lasagna. A dollar here, $5.00 there, $10.00 from over there all quickly add up into real savings.

Clothing and shoe prices continue to rise due to skyrocketing cost of raw materials and labor. You can save a lot of money by avoiding fashion fads and sticking with classic designs and styles which can be worn for multiple years. Thrift and second-hand stores can be a haven for parents of small children who seem to outgrow clothes every 3 or 4 months. One family I know has a net worth of several million dollars. They have 6 boys. When the eldest gets new jeans, they are always 1 size too large. After he has grown out of them, his mom carefully washes and mends them, then puts them into the "Jean" closet where she keeps all of the boys' jean in size order. She rarely has to purchase new jeans for any of her other sons.

TRANSPORTATION

Transportation expenses include all of the following:

- Vehicle payment (including recreational and sports vehicles)
- Vehicle insurance
- Vehicle registration
- Vehicle inspection
- Vehicle maintenance (including oil changes, brakes, tires, etc.)
- Bus, train, subway fares
- Gas, diesel
- Parking and tolls

If your transportation expenses are greater than or equal to the recommendation of 15% you want to reduce them. Some suggestions are:

- Do you have more wheels than you need? Consider selling
  your vehicles on which you are making payments and

purchase a car for cash until you get your finances under control.

- Consider carpooling or public transportation.
- Check your vehicle insurance policy. Auto insurance policies cost 14% more in 2023 than they did in 2022. Are you paying for coverage you don't need? Could you make the deductible higher?
- Make sure you maintain the key elements of your car: oil, brakes, tires. Staying on top of these normal maintenance items will help keep major repairs under control.

Transportation Category Detail	Per Pay Period	Monthly Total
Vehicle Payment		
Vehicle Insurance		
Vehicle Registration		
Vehicle Inspection		
Vehicle Maintenance (tune up, tires, brakes, etc.)		
Fuel (gas, diesel, charging, etc.)		
Parking & Tolls		
Bus, train, subway, Uber, etc.		
Other		
TOTAL		

INSURANCES (NOT INCLUDED ELSEWHERE)

You may have some or all of your insurances deducted from your gross pay. Even if you do, you should still include it in your budget if employer provided insurance does not provide you adequate coverage. For example, your employer may provide life insurance only for employees. You may feel the need to have a life insurance policy for your spouse which you will pay directly. Remember: **Insurance is your friend.**

As an individual, the insurance coverages you probably need are:

- Health (hospital, doctor, dental, vision, prescription, etc.)
- Homeowners or renters
- Automobile
- Disability (short term and long term)
- Life
- Liability
- Long Term Care

Insurance coverage you may not need but may want include:

- Mortgage life insurance
- Accident insurance
- Insurance on outstanding credit card balances
- Travel/Flight insurance
- Cancer/Catastrophic insurance
- Pet Insurance
- Computer/Valuables Insurance

In general, however, your total spending on insurances should not exceed 3% of your net income in order to have a balanced budget.

Insurance Category Detail	Per Pay Period	Monthly Total
Life Insurance		
Homeowner's/Renter's Insurance		
Property Insurance		
Vehicle Insurance		
Disability Insurance		
Funeral/Burial Insurance		
Liability Insurance		
Long Term Care Insurance		
Other		
TOTAL		

HEALTHCARE

Even though there is a federal law "requiring" everyone to have medical insurance, it is not equitable, nor is it enforced. It also does not cover all of the healthcare cost people incur such as dental and vision. The Affordable Care Act was designed to resemble original Medicare. Medicare was never designed to cover 100% of the costs of one's medical expenses. The average annual deductible for a medical policy obtained through the marketplace is $6,500. Therefore, a spending plan that does not include out of pocket healthcare expenses would be incomplete.

You may be one of those people who is never sick. You may have children who are never sick. But what happens when you get a call from the school telling you your child has just fallen off the monkey bars and broken their arm? Do you have the money to pay for your co-pay portion of the medical care your child needs without going into debt? If you have budgeted AND ACCRUED unused portions of your medical budget, you will be prepared.

People with disabilities tend to earn significantly less than others doing comparable work and have significantly more expenses. When an accident or illness comes mid career it's very difficult to make the necessary financial adjustments because so much more of one's income goes towards medical and medical related expenses than previously. Often there are changes and modifications needed to their living environment which are not covered by healthcare insurance. Something as basic as handrails or ramps for safe ingress and egress can cost thousands of dollars.

Approximately one third of those who file bankruptcy, do so because of medical debts. Doctors and hospitals are among the first to turn unpaid bills over to collection agencies which negatively impacts your credit score. While some catastrophic injuries and illnesses could not be predicted, much of the outstanding medical debt results from inadequate medical insurance and/or budgeted and saved funds for deductibles and co-pays. When all of the elements of medical care and services are considered, it is recommended 5% of your net income be set aside for medical expenses. This is above medical insurance premiums you may pay.

Healthcare Category Detail	Per Pay Period	Monthly Total
Dentist/Orthodontist		
Doctor (inc. Co-Pay)		
Hospital and Lab Fees		
Eyeglasses		
Medication		
Medical Equipment/Devices		
Physical, Occupational, & Other Therapies		
OTC Medications, Vitamins, etc.		
Medical and First Aid Supplies		
Other		
TOTAL		

If you want to try to reduce the cost of medications, check out discounts offered by GoodRx, (www.goodrx.com), other prescription discount programs, and online pharmacies such as Cost Plus Drugs, https://costplusdrugs.com/.

EDUCATION

The education budget covers all educational programs for which you must spend funds in order to participate. For the normal family, the education budget should not exceed 1.5% of the family net income. In circumstances in which the family decides to spend more than 1.5% on education, cuts should be made in other categories.

Millions of dollars in scholarships and tuition assistance funds are not disbursed each year simply because no one applies for them. It takes time to search for and apply for these funds. It's actually easier to apply for and receive a student loan. Go to Chapter 23 to see where you might be able to find financial assistance for education.

Education Category Detail	Per Pay Period	Monthly Total
Tuition		
Books, Supplies, Lab Fees		
Uniforms		
Tutor		
Exams & Application Fees		
Sport/Enrichment Camps		
Extracurricular Activities & Lessons		
Other		
TOTAL		

If you need to reduce your spending in the education category, consider cutting the extracurricular activities and lessons such as cheerleading, music lessons, football camp, computer camp, etc. as all of these are discretionary expenditures. Money can be saved on books by using the public or school library where books can be checked out at no cost or by purchasing used books. Private, personal libraries are a luxury.

DEBT PAYMENTS

If you must have debt, your total monthly debt payments should not exceed 10% of your net monthly income. If you have debt, not repaying your debt is not an option. Depending upon the amount of debt you have, you may need to reduce the amount of income allocated to other categories until your debt payments do not exceed 10% of your net monthly income.

Debt Payments Category Detail	Per Pay Period	Monthly Total
Alimony/Child Support		
Chapter 13 Payments		
Court Fines/Garnishments/Judgements		
Credit Cards		
Federal Income Tax		
State Income Tax		
Other Taxes		
Student Loans		
Healthcare (i.e. Dental) Loans		
401K/IRA Loans		
Investment/Margin Loans		
Signature Loans		
Utility/Energy Loans		
Post Dated Check Loan		
Debt Consolidation Loan		
Other		
TOTAL		

HOUSEHOLD GOODS

The purchase of household goods such as appliances, HD televisions and other electronics, furniture, and all of the "little" items purchased for homes such as linens, light features, dishes, pots and pans, etc. can cost thousands of dollars every year – especially if you like your home to look like it was professionally decorated. My brother-in-law will not hang anything – including "works of art" by his 5-year -old grandchild - unless it has been properly matted and framed. You and I may have duct-taped this young Picasso in training's gift to the side of the refrigerator, but not his grandfather.

If not carefully managed, spending on household goods can quickly put you into debt. My 20-year-old dishwasher broke down on Thanksgiving Day. A month later, my 20-year-old water heater quit working the day before Christmas. I can tell by the sound that my clothes dryer is on its last legs. Logically I know everything has a certain life expectancy, but the financial sting of having to replace multiple high-ticket appliances in a short period of time is still there. Yes, some major ticket items can be purchased second hand, but caution is the watchword.

Spending on household goods should not exceed 1.5% of your net monthly income. If you have no debt, the funds budgeted towards debt payment could be added to the allocation for household goods when major purchases are needed.

Household Goods Category Detail	Per Pay Period	Monthly Total
Major Appliances		
Electronics		
Furniture		
Household Repairs and Services		
Piano inc. tuning		
Small Kitchen Appliances		
General Household Items		
Linens, Window Treatments, Rugs		
Interior Decorator, Decorations		
Other		
TOTAL		

PETS AND ANIMALS

Pets can play an important role in one's life by providing companionship, teaching responsibility for the care of one of God's creations, and encouraging physical activity. For most families, pets and animals are not necessary, but are important members of the "family." Therefore, they should be included in your spending plan, but not more than 0.5% of your net income.

Suburban backyard chickens, turkeys, and other fowl are more common today than they were ten years ago. You really can taste the difference between a freshly laid egg and eggs purchased at the grocery store. Humans are not the only creatures who enjoy both feathered and shelled poultry. If you're going to include livestock in your spending plan, you need to include the means to protect them as much as possible.

Service Animals may require a larger budget since a Service Animal is more of a "need" than a "want."

Pets and Animals Category Detail	Per Pay Period	Monthly Total
Feed & Supplies		
Veterinary & Medicine		
Training		
Doggie Daycare, Boarding, etc.		
Pet/Animal Grooming		
Licenses		
Pet/Animal Purchase		
Breeding Fees		
Fencing, Shelter, Doggie Door, etc.		
Other		
TOTAL		

ENTERTAINMENT

For the most part, the entertainment in our lives falls into Maslow's third and fourth levels of hierarchy: Love/Belonging and Esteem. Peer pressure and great media marketing really play on your emotions and are the biggest area of impulse spending. "Honey, let's go to a movie tonight" or "I don't feel like cooking. Let's go out to eat." All of the ESPN channels may seem important especially during football season, but most of the major games can be seen on free network television without the premium costs. It could be argued that some of the details listed in the Entertainment table below are educational – like museums and national parks – or facilitate familial bonding.

I have fond memories growing up in the San Francisco Bay area and annual family outings to Stanford University football games preceded by tailgate lunches in the Eucalyptus Grove. During the Spring and Summer, we'd go to the DeYoung Museum and botanical gardens in Golden Gate Park, followed by a dinner at one of San Francisco's 5-star restaurants. We attended the symphony, fell in love with live theater, and learned not to fall asleep at the opera. I have no idea how much my parents spent on these family activities, but I know they weren't free.

Like so many items on which we spend money, it's very subjective. My parents loved college football. My father grew up in a culturally affluent family. It was important their children be exposed to and have an appreciation for fine arts, the humanities, eclectic foods, and football.

When planning how much you are going to spend on entertainment, it is recommended you spend no more than 0.5% of your net income. This is one of those areas where it is very easy to overspend and go into debt.

Entertainment Category Detail	Per Pay Period	Monthly Total
Television Streaming, Cable, etc.		
Country Club		
Recreational Vehicles, ATV, etc.		
Sports Equipment		
Sporting Events		
Sporting Leagues & Clubs		
Water Crafts		
RV/Boat Storage		
Dining Out & Night Clubs		
Movies & Live Theater		
Video/Computer Games		
Music, Dances, Concerts		
Museums, Zoos, Botanical Gardens		
Recreational & Theme Parks		
Casinos & Racetracks		
Vacations		
Other		
TOTAL		

GIFTS AND DONATIONS

Generally speaking, financial advisors say the amount you spend on gifts and donations should not exceed 0.5% of your net income. You will need to carefully manage this category – which requires a high level of self-discipline.

Guilt perpetuated by family and friends and enhanced by aggressive consumer marketing, especially during holidays, is hard to deflect. Big spending non holidays reveal our need for visual displays to show we are both loved and love. Referring back to Maslow's third and fourth tiers - Love and Belonging, and Emotions – the National Retail Federation reported the average person spent $200 on Valentine's Day in 2023.

This $26 billion spent by Americans goes beyond Cupid. A large bouquet of red roses was sent to a newly hired office receptionist. The card read, "I love you so much! Your Stud" Everyone who passed her desk admired the arrangement. Some stopped and inhaled their fragrance. A few commented on how extravagant the sender had been. No one knew that Stud was her dog. She wanted people to think there was someone special in her life who cared enough to send an expensive showy display.

Does your Stud enjoy the regular services of a dog walker? Do you have a doorman? If you live in a part of the country in which year-end service tips are expected as a part of normal living and/or business, they too need to be included in this category.

Gifts & Donations Category Detail	Per Pay Period	Monthly Total
Children's Allowances		
Holidays, Birthdays, Weddings		
United Way		
Other Non-Profit Donations		
Estate Planning Gifts		
Year End Service Tips		
Other		
TOTAL		

MISCELLANEOUS PROFESSIONAL SERVICES

Only 0.5% of your net income should be allocated to the miscellaneous category for most families. Almost everyone will need an attorney at some point in their life to help with wills and other non-criminal legal matters. Financially free people take counsel from subject matter experts such as tax professionals and financial advisors. In this digital world in which we live, most of us do a very poor job of protecting ourselves from cybercrime and identity theft. Membership in professional organizations is important for employment development and networking. This section also provides a place in your spending plan for you to exercise your constitutional right to bear arms with proper licensing and training.

Misc. Professional Services Category Detail	Per Pay Period	Monthly Total
Spyware, Security Monitoring		
Attorney		
Tax Professional		
Financial Planner/Advisor		
Marriage, Family & Other Counseling		
Professional Organizations		
Firearms Licenses		
Professional Licenses		
Other		
TOTAL		

OTHER

This section contains a lot of spending items that don't really fit into any of the other categories. Most of the items in this category are purely discretionary. However, laundry and dry cleaning and personal grooming may be examples of needs, especially if you are job hunting. This category should not exceed 0.5% of your net income.

Other Category Detail	Per Pay Period	Monthly Total
Burial Plot		
Dry Cleaning/Laundry Services		
Gym/Health Club, Spa/Massage		
Storage Unit		
Jewelry		
Maid/Housecleaning Services		
Personal Grooming, Salon Services		
Subscriptions not included elsewhere		
Dues		
Lottery, Gambling, Gaming		
Tobacco, Alcohol, Recreational Drugs		
Tattoos, Piercings, Other Body Art		
Collectables		
Pictures, Artwork inc. frame & supplies		
Hobby Supplies not included elsewhere		
Other		
TOTAL		

WEEK 15
TRACKING EXPENDITURES

"It frees you from doing things you dislike. Since I dislike doing nearly everything, money is handy." —Groucho Marx

---

Think back to last week. How much money did you spend? What was it for? If you can't remember, think back to yesterday. How much money did you spend yesterday? Did you spend any money on meals or a snack? Did you stop at a gas station or convenience store? Did you wash your vehicle or go to the dry cleaner? Did you order anything online? Did you have a co-pay at the doctor's office or pick up anything at the pharmacy? Did you give your kids money for any reason? It is so easy to go through a day on auto pilot without paying any attention to how much money we unconsciously spend.

In order to be financially free, we need to make conscious spending decisions – and teach our children to do the same. Is the money being spent in pursuit of one of your goals? Is the expenditure unexpected because "life happens" or because you can't say "No"? How many times do you get cash from an ATM or cash back at the grocery store, spend it and then have no idea where it all went? Can you relate to Ben?

Ben always kept $200 in his wallet because "you never know when you're going to need some cash." Wednesday night was Ben's night with his children. His standard practice was to pick them up after work and take them to dinner.

They frequently went to Chuck E Cheese not because the pizza was good, but because his children liked to play the games. It was not uncommon for Ben to spend $100-$120 there. After taking his children back to their mother's house, Ben would usually stop at an ATM on his way home to replenish his wallet.

Ben also had his children every other weekend. Ben usually spent $200-$300 each weekend on the children between food and other items they needed. Invariably one of them needed something for a school project or shoes or a new pair of jeans. Even though Ben paid his ex-wife family support every month, it was easier just to buy the item the kids needed than getting into another argument with their mother about what "family support" was supposed to cover.

Ben was not into online banking, so each month when his bank statement arrived, he would clean out his car looking for the ATM and shopping receipts. He usually found most of them. If he was able to balance his checkbook within $10 of the bank statement, he called it "good" and adjusted his balance to tie to the bank statement.

How does one keep track of all expenditures? By either getting receipts for every single purchase and/or by writing down every penny spent, including vending machines, and drinks purchased when you fill up the car with gas. To some, this may seem extreme. However, most people are not aware of how much they actually spend on incidentals.

One man who started keeping track of every penny he spent was shocked to find he spent $6 – $10 a day on cokes, seven days a week. He was addicted to coke, much like some people are addicted to tobacco or coffee. By tracking his actual expenditures, he realized he could purchase a nice cooler for his office and several cases of cokes for about a quarter of what he had been spending. The money he was no longer spending on cokes could be placed into savings or used to pay down debt.

Another time when people don't realize how much they are spending is when there is unexpected turmoil in their life.

Peggy Sue had never held a "real" job. She had never been solely responsible for every penny that came in and went out of her household. As a student, she had worked part-time and summers in stores carrying the clothes she liked to buy so she could purchase them at a discount.

Peggy Sue married George, an Army officer, a few days after she graduated from college. Peggy Sue's life was dedicated to raising their three children, supporting her husband, and being an active volunteer in their communities and church. They moved frequently in order to spend as much time together as a family as possible.

While Peggy Sue and George discussed finances on a regular basis, George kept the family's financial records. In his mind he was the bread winner therefore he was responsible for making sure the family's needs were taken care of. The only exception to this was when George was deployed to war zones. Peggy Sue kept the family's financial records during those periods.

When George retired from active duty, he and Peggy Sue purchased their first home. They selected an elegant 2 bedroom plus office home in an exclusive "Active Adult" community for people 45 and older near Monterey, California. Many of the residents of the community were also retired military. The community included golf courses, a country club with restaurant and pro shop, a day spa, bike and jogging trails, swimming pools, craft center, a gas station with convenience store, a Starbucks, a dry cleaner, deli, and a bank. They were only 30 minutes away from the restaurants and shops of Carmel and the sands of the Pacific Ocean. George would occasionally enjoy deep sea fishing out of the Monterey marina. George was head of the trauma team at Monterey County Hospital. Peggy Sue volunteered once a week at the local VA hospital. They played bridge weekly at the country club. George golfed at least once a week. Peggy Sue enjoyed the day spa every week. They explored new hobbies at the craft center. They each drove late model vehicles. With their children living on their own, they were enjoying life. They didn't seem to have a care in the world.

Shortly after the fall of Baghdad, the U.S. Army recalled George to active duty. Before being deployed, they prepared a new budget based upon the change of income. George arranged for automatic deposit of his pay and automatic withdrawals for their mortgage, home owner's association dues, insurances, car payments, and internet. Without his income from the hospital, money would be tight, but they felt they would be able to manage without using too much of their savings during his one year assignment. Three months later, George was killed in Iraq. He was 51 years old.

Intellectually, Peggy Sue had always known that George might be killed in the line of duty, but she was unprepared for the financial consequences of his death. Peggy Sue did not think they lived extravagantly. During George's deployment, if she ran out of money before she ran out of month, she withdrew a small amount from their savings. When George died, she realized that even with the survivor's benefit she received, she needed to go to work if she was to maintain her current lifestyle and residence. Peggy Sue hoped her degree in mathematics would help her get a good job. In the meantime, she started tracking every penny she spent. She also recorded all of the fixed payments automatically withdrawal from their bank account.

Peggy Sue put a small notepad in her wallet. Each time she paid cash for anything, she saw the notepad and wrote down what she purchased and how much she paid for it. It didn't matter if it was just a cup of coffee. If she purchased an item with her credit or debit card, she kept the receipt. If she wrote a check or used a debit card, she immediately recorded the amount and the payee in the check register. Every Saturday evening, she entered all of the information from her notepad, receipts, and check register into her computer.

At the end of a month, she reviewed all of her expenditures. The next thing Peggy Sue did was to group her expenditures into the same categories she and George had created for their budget and compare them. It was tedious, but she knew it had to be done.

Peggy Sue was shocked at how much she had spent without putting anything into the savings accounts. She had not needed any new clothes. She had not eaten all of the food in the cupboards and freezer. She had enough soap and shampoos to last for several months. Even though she was used to being alone, she didn't like being at home by herself anymore and jumped at every opportunity to eat out or have coffee with friends. She also spent a lot more time at the craft center. She knew she spent more on gifts than she should have, but how often does your grandbaby have his first birthday? At her son's insistence, Peggy Sue had retained the services of an attorney even though the Army provided many of the same services for free.

It was time for changes. Everything about her life had to be re-examined. Why was she still paying for George's car? Why hadn't she sold it? She didn't play golf, so did she want to remain in the retirement home they had selected together instead of moving closer to her children and grandchildren? How far was she willing to commute to work? At age 50, Peggy Sue had total responsibility for her financial stability and future.

Peggy Sue sought assistance and counseling as she re-evaluated her financial status and future. She set goals which included being debt free, building up her savings account, and obtaining gainful employment. She listed her needs and wants. She evaluated alternatives as she considered her resources. She prioritized her needs and wants. Finally, Peggy Sue was ready to create a new budget.

Through contacts she had made as a volunteer at the VA Hospital, Peggy Sue got a part time job in administration. She would start out earning a net of approximately $540 a week. With her earnings and the funds she would receive from the Army and her husband's estate, her total net monthly income would be $6,293.

Peggy Sue opened several small savings accounts into which she would deposit monies to accrue for home maintenance, home decorating, car maintenance, car insurance, car registration, professional services, vacations, and gifts. She decided she would be more likely to stick to her budget if she put money into separate, specific accounts rather than all into one account. When she pays for one of these items, such as a gift, she will withdraw the amount from the specified account. She took both cars and traded them in for a less expensive car. With $1,200 which she withdrew from her savings account, she had clear title to the car. Peggy Sue also decided she would stay in her home but because George would no longer be around to make minor repairs and improvements, she would need to save more money to pay for repairs and maintenance when they were needed. Additionally, she decided to pay off most of the mortgage with the lump sum survivor's payment she received from the Army. After the refinance, her mortgage, property tax and insurance payment was reduced to $1,000 a month on a 15 year note. She would own the house free and clear by the time she was 65.

Oh, how she missed George. Even though they made financial decisions together, he had always taken care of the details. Now she had to take charge. For the next 3 months Peggy Sue continued to track all of her expenditures. She also took the time she needed to come to a better understanding of the factors influencing her spending. She sought the services of professionals to fully understand the various investments George had established. She knew it would take time, but she was not going to be taken advantage of like some of the widows she knew.

Nearly fifteen years have passed since Peggy Sue became a widow. She has changed her goals and priorities several times and revised her budget accordingly. Even without working, she has a good income stream. She has gained new levels of confidence. Over the years she became more involved with her church community making the decision to go to Africa and teach math in a mission school. She returned for a few months ago to visit her children and grandchildren. She is currently considering selling her home in California and moving closer to her children who now live in Colorado and Texas. She is also thinking about going back to Africa to teach for another year.

WEIRD BUT GREAT INCOME STREAMS YOU CAN DO FROM VIRTUALLY ANYWHERE

"Money won't create success, the freedom to make it will." —*Nelson Mandela*

Do you remember the old adage, *necessity is the mother of invention*? What about *there's got to be a better way* and/or *build a better mouse trap*? If you're the type of person who likes working for someone else doing exactly what they want you to do in exchange for a specific compensation, this principle may not be for you. On the other hand, if you are determined to become financially free and loose the shackles of indebtedness, this may be your favorite principle. It can definitely be one of the most fulfilling.

I know a young man who hated school – primarily because he felt it stifled his creative juices. His parents and sisters were college graduates. Formal academics and the pursuit of higher learning were extremely high priorities in his mother's extended family. There were doctors, lawyers, ambassadors, university professors, and university presidents among his living relatives – and had been in prior generations. This young man almost failed a class during his first semester of college for failing to show the mathematical equation and calculation used in an assignment. When the professor asked him to explain how he derived his answer, he responded, "Google.com. Why should I have to spend time working through the math when I can the answer online?"

In the course of making a case for dropping out of college, he created a list of in-demand jobs not requiring a college degree, which could be performed almost anywhere, and could provide a decent income. The top five on his list were:

1. Plumber
2. Heating, Vent, Air Conditioning Repair
3. Realtor
4. Sound Engineer
5. Junk Collector, Recycler

Watching a few episodes of the television show *Shark Tank* provides ample evidence of the fact that one is limited only by one's imagination when it comes to generating revenue. As at least one shark reminds viewers each episode, self-employment requires commitment and isn't for everyone.

The term "side hustle" is the current euphemism for a second, part time job. With more corporations opting for a 4-day work week, you may have more time to pursue a lucrative side hustle. YouTube is full of people explaining how they are earning $10,000 per month renting out their cars, trucks, and recreational vehicles, and how you too can become a real estate mogul with no cash and lousy credit. Yet as strange as it sounds, there is some truth to these absurd claims.

I've scanned the blogs and publications of organizations such as AARP, SoFi, NerdWallet, iSay, and others to see what "side hustles" they have vetted. (Note: All of money-generating opportunities I've listed are legitimate and legal.) Some of my favorites are:

- Renting Your Backyard for Campers: No matter where you live, if you're in a house, your lawn could be a sought-after destination for adventurers and budget vacationers. Websites like Hipcamp allow you to advertise a comfortable, affordable place to stay for a couple of nights for backpackers or vanlifers.

- Be a Professional Sleeper: Sleep is mysterious to us, and the scientific community has much to research about it. To find gigs, set up some search-engine alerts with keywords such as "sleep study" or "sleep tester" and also comb job boards, especially at universities doing research

- Cleaning Pet Poop for Others: Pet owners without the time or physical ability to clean up after their beloved animals can make good use of your services. All you need is transportation and cleanup equipment to get started. You can build your clientele base by posting flyers around your neighborhood or advertising online. Consider charging between $40 and $100 to clean up a messy yard.

- Renting Out a Shed, Garage or Attic: An app like Neighbor lets you rent out your extra storage space for other people's possessions, processes payments for your services, and is free to use.

- Befriending a Stranger: If you're personable and love embarking on new experiences, being a professional friend may be right for you. RentAFriend.com is a website helping those lacking companionship. Whether you're walking through a park or attending an evening event, your job is to spend time with people looking for friendship, make interesting conversation, and let your personality shine. Rates typically range from $10 to $50 an hour.

- Being a Test Subject: Looking for more crazy ways to earn money? By participating in market research, psychology studies, and more, you can turn your spare time into profitable experiences where you can reap the financial rewards.

- Waiting in Line for Someone: While it's boring when doing this for yourself, waiting in line in someone else's place can be a profitable side hustle. Apps like Spotter or TaskRabbit allow you to connect with customers looking for someone to wait in line for a concert ticket, new tech gadget, or parking permit renewal. The more popular the event or product, the more you can charge.

- Professional Eating: Local restaurants often feed people who are willing to help the restaurant test new menu items, train staff, or accomplishing food challenges. Major League Eating hosts food challenges across the United States with cash prizes for winners.

- Host City Tours: If you live in a town that attracts tourists, you can conduct tours for visitors. You might have a passion for your city's beloved parks or knowledge of its history. Whatever your specialty, you can build a website advertising your services or use an app like Showaround or FreeTour (where you earn money via tips) to put your skills to work.

- Recycling Cans, Glass, Cardboard, Corkscrews, Plastic, Paper, etc: If you're willing to get your hands dirty and invest in a few tools that will save your back from a lot of unnecessary bending, you will provide a great public service cleaning up roadside trash as well as earn a few dollars for yourself or your favorite charity. College dorms and apartments are a great place to find cardboard especially on move-in days. Many businesses may also allow you to collect and recycle their throwaways as long as you don't interfere with their customer foot traffic.

- Recycle Electronics, Cell Phones, Rechargeable Batteries, Printer Ink Cartridges, etc.: You need to research what is allowed to be disposed of in your area because some electronics contain hazardous materials and can't be disposed of in your regular trash or recycling. Many cell phone providers like AT&T and Verizon will give you a gift card or vouchers for a phone you're no longer using. These can be used toward purchasing a new product.

- Recycling Golf and Tennis Balls: Millions of golf and tennis balls get tossed out as garbage in the U.S. every year, but you might be able to make some money on them by cleaning and packaging gently used balls.

With a little research and effort, you can turn your used and unwanted items into extra money. Recycling items can be a big win for your pocketbook and the planet. Whether you focus on collecting cans, unwanted clothes, cardboard, or corks, you can wind up with some extra cash while doing good. The following list are a few websites through which you may be able to sell pretty much anything including items you make like keychains, eccentric jewelry, or clothes.

- Facebook Marketplace
- Amazon
- eBay
- OfferUp
- Poshmark
- Etsy
- thredUP
- eBid
- Bookoo
- Vinted
- Vestiaire Collective
- LePrix
- TheRealReal
- Rebag
- Bag Borrow or Steal
- Once Wed
- PreOwnedWedding
- DeCluttr
- Gazelle

Most financial gurus recommend multiple streams of income in order to weather economic turbulence. They usually advocate passive income which is income that doesn't require much hands-on involvement. However, most passive income requires significant financial investment. Once you're well on the road to financial freedom, out of debt, with 3 – 6 months living expenses in a liquid savings account, building long term passive income streams is a great addition to your personal financial plan. When you are ready to start earning passive income, you might consider non-traditional as well as traditional investments such as:

- Solar panels on your roof or land
- Cellular pole/panels on your land
- Wind turbines on your land

SECTION 4 – FINANCIALLY AT PEACE WITH THE WORLD AND GOD

"Money in its proper place is a worthwhile and necessary instrument for a well-rounded life, but when it is projected to the status of a god it becomes a power that corrupts and an instrument of exploitation." —Martin Luther King Jr.

You no longer feel guilty about money you do or don't have. You no longer care about what anyone outside of your family thinks about your personal financial management. You are at peace with yourself and your God.

Allow yourself 3 weeks to complete Section 4. The ***Financially Free in 23 Weeks Stewardship Workbook*** is a weekly guide designed to help you apply the structural foundation and principles you're about to learn.

LIFE HAPPENS

"If inflation continues to soar, you're going to have to work like a dog just to live like one." —George Gobel

---

Why do most budgets fail? For the same reason most diets fail and most New Year resolutions fail: Lack of a plan; lack of commitment; lack of support. But there are times when even with a plan, commitment, and support a person's budget will fail because life happens. What does your faith teach about preparing for life's unexpected events?

When "life" happens, budgets and the goals they supported need to be immediately reexamined. While it is sometimes difficult to recognize when conditions in the work place, in one's family, or with one's personal health are beginning to change for the worse, signs can often be seen in a detailed analysis of expenditures.

Ed and Monica were hard working small business owners. Ten years ago, after being laid off from a high-tech company for the second time, Ed decided he wanted to be in control of his own financial destiny. Their children were grown, so their felt as though stepping out on their own would not be too risky. If they didn't like it, they could always return to corporate America.

Together they created goals and priorities. They conducted extensive research and analysis of various opportunities they thought would help them reach their goals. At the same time, they created, and stuck to, a very strict budget so they could save the money they needed to start their own business.

Even though they had always worked for national technology corporations, they decided to purchase a fast-food franchise and opened a new location in a rapidly expanding part of town. The money they had saved paid their startup costs and their living expenses for the first 6 months of operations. Revenue at the original restaurant was growing at a slow, but steady pace. After a couple of years, they opened two more locations in neighboring towns. It took almost five years for all three stores to be operating in the black.

Ed and Monica had subsidized the stores' occasional cash shortages with the balance of their savings and with credit card debt. They both worked full time in their stores. During the pandemic they managed to keep all of their locations open by quickly focusing on cheerful delivery with bright balloon bouquets attached to their bags. They took out an SBA Payroll Protection Plan loan to keep from having to lay off employees. As the shutdowns eased, supply chain problems continued and costs really started to increase.

They always managed to pay their employees, vendors, mortgages, and the minimum amount due on their credit cards, but the stores were not making enough money to enable Ed and Monica to pay themselves full salaries or to save any money. If they could open two more stores, they would be able to purchase supplies at a volume discount and have money left to start replenishing their savings account. A year ago, they opened their fourth store and planned to open a fifth location this year.

As small business owners, Ed and Monica had tried unsuccessfully to find medical insurance they could afford. Since the majority of their employees were part-time, they were not required by law to provide health insurance coverage to their employees. They wanted to offer them an option, but due to their size they did not qualify for good group policy.

The only medical insurance Ed and Monica had for themselves was a catastrophic policy.

Three months ago Ed got sick, but thought it was just a bad case of the stomach flu. After several days, he agreed to go to the doctor who sent him to the hospital for an emergency appendectomy. Ed had to spend a week in the hospital after the surgery on IV antibiotics to treat the infection caused by his acute appendicitis.

Ed was surprised when the health insurance company said an appendectomy was not considered a catastrophic medical event and therefore denied coverage. He asked the hospital and doctors if he could make payment arrangements because he did not have $42,000 readily available to pay the total amounts due. Some said he could make regular monthly payments, others said he could not.

Ed and Monica took the $12,000 they had set aside for the fifth store and paid the anesthesiologist and part of the hospital bill. The hospital, surgeon, infectious disease doctor, and hospitalist were requiring minimum payments totaling $833 a month for the next 3 years.

Monthly cash flow from the four stores was not always sufficient to accommodate this additional financial burden. They had only been able to make 5 monthly payments before their "slow" season started. Last month Ed and Monica were only able to send $50 to the hospital and $25 each to the three doctors. Yesterday, they received a notice stating their account with the surgeon had been turned over to a collection agency. If the account was not paid in full within 15 days, a judgment would be sought in civil court.

As Ed spoke to his attorney today, he was advised to immediately file Chapter 13 Bankruptcy protection in order to prevent the collection agency from trying to garnish funds from any of his business accounts. His attorney also told him this would also buy him time to work out an acceptable remedy.

Prior to his appendicitis, the last time Ed had been in a hospital was when he tore his knee up playing football in college. "I remember laughing at the Aflac commercials aired during football games," Ed recounted. I remember telling my roommate, "I never thought I'd be the duck on crutches. Good thing the school's insurance is covering this." Thirty years later, none of that seems funny anymore.

When life throws you a curveball, what do you do? Call time out. Go back to the basics. Find a quiet spot where you and your family can spend uninterrupted time in prayerful contemplation. Reexamine the goals and priorities you have set. Revise them as needed. There is nothing wrong with changing the direction in which you are heading. Just the opposite. If external forces – be they health, inflation, war, whatever – knocks you off balance, it **IS** okay to make changes. In fact, sometimes a drastic change is the best thing you can do in order to be financially free.

DISASTER PLANNING

"The only reason I made a commercial for American Express was to pay for my American Express bill." —Peter Ustinov

---

Disasters can happen at any time, anywhere, to anyone. Disasters can be man-made, results of nature, or a combination. Some disasters may affect only a few people. Others may impact millions. A disaster may be a fire, a hurricane, a death, a divorce, or a myriad of other disruptive events. They may be preceded with numerous warnings, or they may strike without any notice.

My first encounter with a major disaster was the San Francisco Loma Prieta earthquake in 1989. Having grown up near San Francisco, I had experienced many smaller earthquakes. I knew the safety precautions to take, such as shutting off the gas and where to shelter as aftershocks hit. I had a supply of bottled water, (a rarity back then), for safe drinking, flashlights with extra batteries, and a supply of food that required little or no cooking. However, I was not prepared for the extended power outages that accompanied this earthquake. Street lights and traffic control lights stopped working making driving hazardous. Those who did try to drive were not able to fill their vehicles with gas because gas pumps weren't working.

The most inconvenient part of this earthquake, (at least for me), was the fact that computers weren't working for three days. That meant payroll was delayed. I was living paycheck to paycheck. As soon as the telephone lines were available, I was on the phone calling my creditors asking for a late fee waiver, until I got paid. When I received my paycheck, I immediately started putting a few dollars into "the cookie jar," and continued to do so every payday.

Technology and disaster recovery systems have dramatically changed since 1989. Unfortunately, the frequency and severity of disasters have also increased. Working with survivors of Hurricane Katrina, I created the following Survivors' Toolkit to help people be better prepared to prevent unnecessary financial loss following a disaster. Drawing from lessons learned, this chapter is to help you organize and accomplish the many tasks suddenly needed to protect you and your family from further financial losses. Experience has shown that it is often the little things that cause the biggest problems down the road, so I've tried to include a lot of minutiae you might not have thought of doing. This is not a complete list because everyone's situation is a little bit different, but it will make it a bit easier for you to financially survive a major disaster should you ever need to.

DISASTER SURVIVOR'S TOOLKIT

The first thing to do is prepare a 72-Emergency kit for each person in your family. This kit should contain the bare minimum food, water and supplies you need to survive on your own until you can get help. The best resource for a detailed list is www.ready.gov. Remember to include medicines needed by each member of your family. Keep your prepacked emergency kits in a location where they are easy to grab and go if you have to evacuate. Consider keeping some items permanently in your vehicle.

If you get discouraged, remember help is available, but you and you alone are in control of your money and personal financial situation going forward to your new normal. **Do not allow anyone to pressure you into signing any agreement or contract without giving you time to read and understand what you are being asked to sign.** Beware of scammers. If it is a good deal today, it will still be a good deal tomorrow. Before you sign anything:

- Ask questions
- Verify licenses, bonds, permits, & other credentials
- Read the fine print

Know before you owe.

If you do not feel like you can cope with the financial challenges you face right now, obtain counseling. It's available to you at no cost. See https://www.samhsa.gov/find-help/disaster-distress-helpline or call the Disaster Distress Help Line at 1-800-985-5990 or text "TalkWithUs" to 66746 to talk to a trained counselor from the National Institutes of Health Substance Abuse and Mental Health Services Administration. Counselors are on call 24/7/365.

REGISTER WITH FEMA

Don't expect FEMA to automatically take care of you. Primary disaster recovery is the responsibility of each state. FEMA comes in only after the state requests them to do so. Once your state has requested FEMA's assistance, you must register with FEMA to find out if you qualify for assistance. To find out what assistance is available for your area, go to: https://www.disasterassistance.gov/. Use the *excellent* resource! Don't reinvent the wheel.

FILE INSURANCE CLAIMS

Make a list of the items lost, damaged, or destroyed due to the disaster. The list does not have to be extremely detailed, but you will have to provide enough information to the insurance company for them to begin processing your claim. Collect the following information to file with all of your appropriate insurance policies, flood, homeowners, vehicle, etc.

- Insurance Co.
- Policy #
- Website
- Property Address
- Name of Adjuster or Contact person
- How will you communicate (i.e. email)
- Instructions from insurance company
- Claim #
- Date

CONTACT ALL UTILITY COMPANIES

Unless you know you're going to be back in your home within a few days, cancel all of your utilities. There are a lot of reasons for doing this, but the one we're most concerned about is you don't want to be charged for using something you aren't using, i.e. you don't want to be charged for electricity at your home when the disaster struck, and also being charged for electricity at a new, though temporary, residence.

Note: Most utility companies will try to transfer services to your new residence but, until you know for sure where you will be living for the next while, you'll have more flexibility to negotiate a lower rate if your current service is **not** transferred. Collect the following information to contact all of your utility companies: electric, gas, water, sewer, satellite/cable, internet, etc.

- Company
- Account #
- Name of person with whom you spoke
- Website
- Is there a security deposit to be applied to the final bill or refunded? If yes, what is the amount?

- Address to which final bill/refund can be sent
- Cancellation #
- Date

MAIL AND DELIVERY SERVICES

Go to www.usps.gov and submit either a "vacation hold" or "forward to new address" for all of your items delivered to you via the U.S. Postal Service.

Do the same thing for everything regularly delivered to your home or business and services that are regularly performed at your home or business, i.e.

- Newspapers
- Medical supplies
- Water
- Propane
- Insect/Pest Control (i.e. Terminex)
- Pool Maintenance
- Yard Maintenance
- Feed (for livestock)
- Food (for people)
- Etc.

Remember, unless you **specifically cancel** the delivery or service, the provider may continue to deliver or attempt delivery and therefore bill you. Failure to pay a bill could create future problems. Collect the following information to track your delivery services.

- Company
- Account #
- Name of person with whom you spoke
- Website
- Is there a security deposit to be applied to the final bill or refunded? If yes, what is the amount?

- Address to which final bill/refund can be sent
- Cancellation #
- Date

CREDIT AND DEBIT CARDS

This is the money management category in which we receive the greatest number of questions and requests for assistance. Again, because every situation is different, the information and recommendations made are designed to be of benefit to the greatest number of survivors.

When physical damage occurs to an item used as collateral for a loan – for example, your vehicle was last seen under a giant oak tree - most loan contracts contain language such as:

"If the [item] is a total loss, you must use the insurance proceeds to pay what you owe us. If your insurance ... doesn't pay all you owe, you must pay what is still owed."

Regardless of whether or not your insurance covers loss or damage to items purchased via installment payments, failure to pay all that you agreed to pay, could result in the lender turning your account over to a collection agency, filing a law suit against you, and/or taking the item and selling it in order to get back the money they lent you to make the original purchase. Examples of items often purchased via installment agreements include, but are not limited to:

- Vehicles
- Appliances
- Furniture
- Electronics

Any change to the current terms and conditions of any debt you currently owe is at the discretion of the creditor. In general you must contact each creditor individually if you want to request:

- Interest rate adjustment
- Late payment penalty fee waiver
- Hardship payment deferral

As mentioned before, check out all of the special waivers, assistance, and other programs being made available from Federal Agencies. These are listed at:

https://www.fema.gov/news-release
https://www.samhsa.gov/find-help/disaster-distress-helpline

Do you have **all** of your credit and debit cards physically with you right now? If not, you should contact the card issuing company, cancel the card as lost due to the disaster, and request a new card.

Pull a copy of your credit report at www.annualcreditreport.com to obtain the account numbers of all of your credit cards (if you don't have them) as well as the contact information for the card issuer.

Contact your bank or credit union to request new debit cards. If you also had physical paper checks no longer in your possession, talk to your bank or credit union about closing the affected checking account and opening a new one.

We also recommend you select a new PIN and change the password on all of your accounts. The following form can be used for all of your creditors. Make sure you keep this information with all of your other disaster-related documents.

Don't forget to check out the special waivers, assistance, and other programs made available from Federal Agencies. These are listed at:

https://www.fema.gov/news-release
https://www.samhsa.gov/find-help/disaster-distress-helpline

- Card Name
- Account Number
- Number of Cards
- Customer Service #

- Date Called
- Cancel?
- Reset PIN?
- New Password?
- Name of person with whom you spoke
- Card Issuer instructions

NEGOTIATING WITH CREDITORS

If you would like to have your interest rate, minimum payment, or other terms and conditions changed in your current agreement with one of your creditors, the following information is designed to help you.

You may not achieve the reductions you seek without consistent follow up with your creditor. You may have to write to your creditor multiple times.

All requests must be in writing sent certified via U.S. Mail, signature required. The signed, return receipt you receive is your proof that your request has been received by your creditor.

All requests should clearly state your account number, your name and address as listed on the account, the desired objectives and should include documentation name, date, and federal identification number of disaster, proof of loss of income and inability to continue payments. Suggested documentation includes (but is not limited to):

- FEMA Assistance Acceptance Notice
- Lay-off/Termination Notice
- Unemployment benefit statement
- Disability benefit statement
- Food Stamp statement
- Current bank statements
- SSA/SSDI benefit statement
- Hospital/medical bill
- List of all household residents, age, income, source of income, and relationship to you
- Tax return

- W-2
- 1099

If you purchased credit card payment insurance or other debt repayment insurance, documentation as specified in your policy will be required before the insurance will kick in. Make sure you understand all of the terms and conditions that would invalidate the coverage, such as continued use of a credit card. **READ THE FINE PRINT!!!!**

When negotiating with governmental agencies, such as the IRS, interest and/or penalties usually continue to accrue even if payments are deferred.

Court ordered payments, i.e. judgments and garnishments, usually require adjustment to the court order by the courts. You should consult your attorney. Judgments and garnishments usually cannot be taken from SSA/SSDI benefits.

Negotiating for changes in your consumer debt usually yields poor results and usually hurts your credit rating. Any time you consider negotiating with a creditor regarding consumer debt, you should do the following:

- Stop using credit card
- Stop using payday loans
- Stop using title loans

If your debt is secured, you should be prepared to lose the collateral, i.e. ATV, refrigerator, HD/Plasma television, etc.

Many creditors will not negotiate with you as long as you are current with your payments. If you are not current with your payments, many creditors will not negotiate with you until you are 6 or more months behind in your payments.

Doctors, hospitals, dentists, medical laboratories, and other medical facilities are especially quick to sell past due accounts to a collection agency once they reach 60 days past due. Make sure you keep copies of all payments made by your insurance company and all payments you have made. Contact your medical provider's financial aid or accounts receivable department immediately if you need to set up payments over time.

Always obtain a written, signed agreement from your creditor for the negotiated settlement. Never allow a creditor to automatically draft a payment from your bank account. If you are considering a debt management plan note:

Debt Management Plans (DMP) are dangerous.

- Many are under Federal investigation
- Most charge high up-front fees
- Most charge monthly fees

ALL Debt Management Plans (DMP) have a negative impact on credit scores.

NEGOTIATING WITH CREDITORS - FAILED ATTEMPTS

Are your attempts to negotiate with your credit card issuer going nowhere fast? Are your phone calls being forwarded to third parties who have no affiliation with your creditor?

If you are one of the hundreds of individuals who are trying to negotiate in good faith with one of your credit card issuers, but the creditor refuses to discuss your case with you, you now have a new advocate. The Consumer Financial Protection Bureau (CFPB) has a web site, www.consumerfinance.gov through which you may file complaints about your credit card issuer.

You should be prepared to provide the following information:

- Credit Card Issuer's Name
- Your account number
- Your name
- Specific, detailed complaint (i.e. specific dates and times in which you attempted to contact your creditor and the specific actions taken by your creditor such as transferring you to a non-affiliated third party)

- Your desired outcome

Note: CFPB will forward all complaints to the credit card issuer allowing them one more opportunity to resolve the problem. If the credit card issuer does not resolve the problem to the consumer's satisfaction, CFPB will work with the consumer to resolve the issue.

PROTECT YOUR IDENTITY

Because your life is temporarily in disarray, unscrupulous individuals may try to take advantage of the fact that you are a bit distracted, and they will try to steal your identity for their own personal gain. To help prevent that from occurring, we recommend placing a notice on your credit report at each of the three major credit bureaus, then freeze your credit report.

Credit reports: The official free site to obtain a copy of your credit report from each of the 3 major credit bureaus is www.annualcreditreport.com. Federal law allows you to get a free copy of your credit report from each of the major credit reporting companies, Equifax, Experian and TransUnion, once every 12 months. Look for accounts you don't recognize and incorrect information (employers, addresses, etc.). There are many similarly named credit report services, but www.AnnualCreditReport.com is the only one that is truly free.

Financial and account information: Check bills and account information immediately. Track mailed statements, new credit cards and printed check orders. Shield ATM pad when entering your password or PIN. Beware of shoulder surfers and eavesdroppers when talking on your cell phone. Shred all documents with your Social Security number before discarding. Notify the Social Security Administration and credit bureaus of the death of a loved one. If you think your driver's license has been compromised, contact the fraud department of your state's DMV to learn your options.

Cell phone/wireless device protection: If your phone is lost or stolen, a strong password will prevent anyone from using it. You should place passwords on your credit card, financial and phone service accounts.

Specialty consumer reports: Consumer reports include not only credit reports but also reports about you made to employers, insurance companies, banks and landlords. Under FCRA rules, you are entitled to a free report every 12 months from all nationwide specialty agencies (those compiling reports for targeted uses).

Whether you rent or own your home, you should check your rental history yearly. ID thieves can gain access to your personal information for the sole purpose of using it to rent an apartment or house. Numerous companies prepare reports for landlords concerning individuals who have applied to rent housing. Here are a few:

- **CoreLogic Rental Properties**: May include criminal and/or landlord-tenant records as well as rental performance history. Call 888-333-2413.
- **Tenant Data:** Provides information not only on rental payment history, but also on personal suitability as a potential resident. Call 1-800-228-1837, or download the form at http://www.tenantdata.com . Mail it with a copy of your Social Security card and a government-issued photo ID, such as a driver's license or passport, to: Personal Report Request, Tenant Data Services, P.O. Box 5404, Lincoln, NE 68505-0404.
- **RentBureau:** Receives rental payment data from its national network of multifamily property management companies. This data is accessed by resident screening companies for use during the rental application process. Order your Rental History Report by using the form available at http://www.experian.com/rentbureau/rental-payment.html (right-hand column), or call 1-877-704-4519.

If you're looking to rent and likely to be subject to a tenant screening, you could ask the landlord/rental agency for the name and contact info for the screening company.

It only takes a day or two before some unscrupulous person is going to try to take advantage of the fact that you've been involved in a major disaster. Therefore, you need to give serious thought to placing a credit freeze and/or a security freeze on your files at all three major credit bureaus.

Credit freeze: A credit freeze will prevent ID thieves from opening up new accounts using your personal information because credit issuers will not be able to access your credit file. In most states, the credit freeze is available at no cost to ID theft victims.

If you place a credit freeze, you will continue to have access to your free annual credit report and you'll also be able to buy your credit report and credit score. Companies with whom you already conduct business–for example, your mortgage, credit card or cell phone companies–will still have access to your credit report as would collection agencies working for one of those companies. Companies will also still be able to offer you prescreened credit (unsolicited credit offers you receive in the mail). And, according to the FTC, in some states potential employers, insurance companies, landlords, and other non-creditors can still get access to your credit report with a credit freeze in place.

If you're married, both you and your spouse must freeze your separate credit files to fully protect your household.

After processing your request, each agency will mail you a confirmation letter and a PIN or password for you to use whenever you temporarily lift the freeze, and if you permanently remove it. In many states, you can choose to lift the freeze for a specific period of time or for a particular creditor or other credit report user. If you temporarily lift the freeze for a particular third party, you will provide a unique access code (TransUnion and Equifax) or your PIN (Experian) to that person or business so they can access your credit report.

Security freeze: A security freeze is a step you take to prevent credit, loans and services from being opened in your name without your permission. You will need to request a freeze with each of the three credit reporting companies. There is no fee for this service. Once you place a security freeze on your credit report, businesses will not be able to obtain a copy of your report in connection with any new applications for credit. Before you apply for new credit, you will need to temporarily lift the security freeze following the procedures from the credit reporting company where you placed the freeze.

To place a security freeze, you must contact each of the credit reporting companies. You can do so online or through the mail.

Types of information you should be prepared with:

- Your full name, including middle initial and suffix, such as Jr., Sr. II, III
- Social Security Number
- Date of Birth
- Current address
- All addresses where you have lived during the past two years
- Email address
- A copy of a government-issued identification card, such as a driver's license or state ID card, etc.
- FEMA Assistance Acceptance Notice
- A copy of a utility bill, bank or insurance statement, etc.

CREATE A WRITTEN BUDGET SPECIFICALLY FOR THIS DISASTER

If you've never created a written budget before, now is the time to start. Equally important, if you've never kept a good record of all of your expenditures, it is critical you start doing so now!

Are you going to:

- Clean up and repair, restore, or rebuild
- Clear out and relocate
- Walk away and forget
- Other

Regardless of the direction you choose, you will have a lot of temporary and unusual expenses during the aftermath of the disaster.

Be prepared to create a new budget **each time** there is a major change in your situation. The following are examples of major changes you may experience:

- Insurance money is received or spent
- Your place of residence changes
- The number of people living at your place of residence changes
- Employment income changes

Because you will be faced with hard decisions every day as you ask yourself, "Is this a *NEED* or a *WANT*", we recommend you include prayer in your decision-making process. You may be surprised at how much goals and priorities can change in a matter of minutes.

Again, if you find yourself struggling to make decisions; if you find yourself doing emotional spending for yourself or your children; if you suddenly ask yourself, "Where has all of the money gone?", STOP what you're doing and get help. Call the Disaster Distress Help Line at 1-800-985-5990 or text "TalkWithUs" to 66746 to talk to a trained counselor from the National Institutes of Health Substance Abuse and Mental Health Services Administration. Counselors are on call 24/7/365.

GETTING HELP WHEN YOU NEED IT

"I made my money the old-fashioned way. I was very nice to a wealthy relative right before he died" —*Malcolm Forbes*

A professor told his students, "I don't expect you to know everything about this subject. That is virtually impossible due to the rapid changes taking place. What I do expect you to know is where to go and how to find the most recent innovations, research, and failures." This advice is especially applicable to your personal financial situation. Too many things can change without warning. No one deliberately plans to tank their own economic well-being. Anxiety sets in when we are so broke that we don't even have a few dollars in our pockets. There is no shame in asking for help. The shame comes when your pride prevents you from admitting you may not know everything.

Governmental assistance varies not only by state, but may also vary by county. The first place to start looking at programs that might be available to you is www.benefits.gov.

The next place to go is www.211.org. A 211 agency connects people with community and government agencies that can provide help. There are more than **200 211 agencies across the United States**, each with a team of community specialists who are available to help you access the best local resources and services to address any need. The 211 network responds to more than **21 million requests for help every year**. Most calls, web chats, and text messages are from people looking for help meeting basic needs like housing, food, transportation, and health care.

States and territories receive funding from the federal government to provide child care financial assistance for low-income families in their state. These programs help low-income families pay for child care so they can work or attend school. Eligibility requirements are different in each state. Go to www. https://childcare.gov/index.php/consumer-education/get-help-paying-for-child-care for more information. You should also check with your employer. Some employers, especially those in blue-collar fields, are beginning to subsidize childcare themselves in a bid to keep workers.

The rising cost of healthcare can lead to significant financial hardship. Some healthcare providers will negotiate the cost with you if you do not have good healthcare insurance. It's a little more difficult with prescription drugs. Many states have State Pharmaceutical Assistance Programs (SPAPs) that help some people pay for prescription drugs based on financial need, age, or medical condition. Each state has their own rules, so check with your State Health Insurance Assistance Program (SHIP) for details. You should also check out discounts offered by GoodRx, (www.goodrx.com), and other prescription discount programs.

If you want to know how much a drug really costs, go to https://costplusdrugs.com/. Cost Plus Drugs is one of Mark Cuban's companies. Mr. Cuban backed the company because he thinks consumers have the right to know the actual cost of a drug, and should be able to obtain needed medications without the markups from middlemen. It's important to know that Cost Plus Drugs focuses on generic drugs, so they do not carry all prescription drugs.

The American Connectivity Program, or ACP, provides a $30 monthly discount on Wi-Fi to qualifying low-income families. Currently, 16 million households are enrolled. The FCC subsidizes broadband access through a program called Lifeline Support. However, it only provides a $9.25 discount. To qualify for the ACP, households must have income at or below 200% of the federal poverty line. With the average cost of basic internet service hovering just over $30, the ACP doesn't just ease a monthly expense, it eliminates it entirely for many.

Each state has a list of registered insurance companies licensed to operate in that state. States also maintain lists of complaints consumers have filed against insurance companies. Click on Company Profiles for information on an insurance company's license status in that state, its financial status, and compliance history.

Some states, such as Texas, offer insurance to uninsurable property owners. The Texas FAIR Plan Association (www.texasfairplan.org) provides residential property insurance to qualified consumers who are having difficulty obtaining coverage from licensed insurance companies.

Education Scholarships and tuition assistance programs are available from both traditional and non-traditional sources. *As with every resource mentioned, there is always the possibility the organization may no longer exist. A few websites we think will be around for a while are:*

- **www.cappex.com** : The scholarship dashboard lets students manage their scholarships by setting a status for each scholarship (Might Apply, Will Apply, Applied, Won, Did Not Win, Doesn't Fit, Will Not Apply).
- **www.chegg.com** : Users can search by their school year, age and GPA and create a personal profile to find better scholarship matches.
- **www.fastweb.com** : The "Featured College Scholarships" section of the website frequently updates scholarship offers most students qualify for.
- **www.petersons.com** : Filter your search by scholarships for college or grad school on this site.
- **www.scholarships.com** : The site allows users to browse by special attributes. For example, users can search for scholarships for people who are adopted, LGBTQ or vegan.

A sampling of companies, unions, and associations who offer tuition assistance to employees/members is shown below. More information can be found at https://getschooled.com/article/5206-companies-with-great-tuition-reimbursement-programs/ and https://collegeguidepost.com/scholarships/best-part-time-jobs-with-tuition-reimbursement/

- Amazon
- Target
- Walmart and Sam's Club
- Hewlett Packard Enterprise Co.
- Starbucks Corp.
- United Auto Workers
- Texas Instruments
- McDonalds
- United Parcel Service, Inc.
- All U.S. Military Branches
- AT&T
- Quick Trip
- Publix
- Papa John's

Formal education isn't for everyone. Some companies, unions, and associations who offer apprenticeships or on-the-job skills training for employees/members:

- Woodward, Inc.
- Kreg Enterprises, Inc.
- Toyota Motor Corp.
- National Association of Manufacturers
- Michelin North America Inc.

The Coronavirus Aid, Relief, and Economic Security Act, also known as the CARES Act, contained a number of programs to "assist" those impacted by the pandemic. These include, but are not limited to, mortgage forbearance, federal student loan forbearance, IRA distributions, and income tax. Most of these have expired, but some are still in limbo.

Go to https://www.consumerfinance.gov/coronavirus to find the current status of the different programs.

Technical Colleges and universities are an underused source of assistance. Students need to be able to practice what they are learning. Under the supervision of a qualified professional/professor, the public can benefit from many free or reduced price services such as:

- Legal Aid
- Dental Hygiene
- Physical Therapy
- Mental Health counseling
- Agriculture and gardening
- Auto mechanics and body work

Public libraries, churches, synagogues, mosques, and community centers are repositories for a vast number of services provided by non-profit organizations and individuals. They offer programs that include:

- Lifelong Literacy, including reading and writing
- Addiction recovery and support
- Language skills including American Sign Language (ASL)
- Computer and technology skills training
- Wellness workshops
- Financial workshops

Whether it is a natural disaster, medical emergency, loss of a job, or a lack of business due to a very slow economy, or a change in your priorities, your personal financial fitness will help determine how well you will be able to weather the financial storms that whirl around each of our lives. If you need it, help is available. More resources can be found at www.financialfreein23.net.

SECTION 5 – NO LONGER COMPLACENT

"Don't save what is left after spending; spend what is left after saving." —Warren Buffet

As you become financially free, you look outward. You become a better steward of all with which God has blessed you. You do a better job of preparing for unexpected events – both minor and catastrophic. You try to stay informed of outside forces that may impact your financial freedom and make sure that all reports made about you are accurate. You are more vigilant of those trying to con you and others. You become actively involved in trying to lift others.

Allow yourself 4 weeks to complete Section 5. The ***Financially Free in 23 Weeks Stewardship Workbook*** is a weekly guide designed to help you apply the structural foundation and principles you're about to learn.

UNDERSTANDING YOUR CREDIT REPORT

"An athlete cannot run with money in his pockets. He must run with hope in his heart and dreams in his head." —Emil Zatopek

---

Consumer credit is becoming more expensive. Credit, when used, must be used wisely.

What exactly is credit? The word credit, as used in reference to financial transactions means "something entrusted to another", according to the Merriam-Webster dictionary. Put in other words, credit is an amount or sum put at someone's disposal by a financial institution or company. Credit is also the time given for payment for goods or services sold on trust.

Good credit is valuable. Having the ability to borrow funds allows us to buy things we would otherwise have to save for years to afford: homes, cars, a college education. Credit is an important financial tool, but it can also be dangerous, leading people into debt far beyond their ability to repay. There are four fundamental rules of the responsible use of consumer credit.

1. A person should never borrow more than 20% of his/her annual net income.
2. A person's monthly debt payments should not exceed 10% of his/her net monthly income.
3. The use of credit should be the exception, not the norm.
4. When credit is obtained, the terms and conditions required by the creditor must be fully understood.

By law, all creditors must disclose in writing what the use of credit is going to cost and must allow you to read all of the terms and conditions on credit card and other loan documents before you sign. Most consumers do not take the time to do this – even when a sales person isn't standing over them urging them to "just sign." Most companies hire attorneys to read the terms and conditions associated with obtaining credit and then negotiate with the creditors if the terms need to be adjusted or clarified. Consumers typically sign the contract without reading past the APR. There may be other terms and conditions which could affect you as much, if not more, than the APR. Are you aware of all of the conditions that allow a creditor to change the rate of interest and/or the monthly minimum you must pay?

In the Security Agreement from RC Willey, it states,

"I am giving you a purchase money security interest in all goods purchased from you, or a participating merchant on credit under this Agreement and all proceeds of such goods. You may exercise any rights granted to a secured party under the provisions of the Uniform Commercial Code, including the right to repossess and sell such goods or proceeds thereof. If the amount received on sale of the goods, less costs of repossession, storage, sale and other costs, is insufficient to pay all amounts I owe you, I agree to pay you the amount of any such deficiency including finance charges and other fees."

Do you know what this means? It means that if you do not make your agreed upon payments on time, the items you purchased on credit can be repossessed. Would you like to have your living room sofa removed from your home? Or your child's bed? Your refrigerator?

Creditors need to be able to generate revenue in order to be profitable. They also need to be able to be compensated for the amount of risk they assume when issuing credit. Due to the increased number of restrictions put on credit institutions, loopholes in the laws and regulations are being found and exploited. For example, federal law prohibits a creditor from terminating an open-end consumer credit plan simply because the consumer has not incurred finance charges on the account. A creditor is allowed to charge the consumer an "Inactivity Fee" if the account is not used.

This means that if you have a credit card which has a zero balance, but the account is open and has not been used for a while, the credit card issuer could charge you a fee for keeping the account open. However, if you use this same credit card and pay the balance in full every month, the issuer cannot charge you a fee even though you did not pay any interest on the account because you paid the balance in full each month.

Because the terms and conditions are changing almost constantly, you need to make sure you read and understand all notices inserted in your monthly account statement. This is part of such a disclosure from Citibank.

"Rates, fees, and terms may change: We have the right to change the rates, fees and terms at any time, for any reason, in accordance with the cardmember agreement and applicable law. These reasons may be based on information in your credit report such as your failure to make payments to another creditor when due, amounts owed to other creditors, the number of credit accounts outstanding or the number of credit inquiries."

The key point in this example of credit terms and conditions you need to remember is that this **bank may increase the amount of interest you are charged if you are late with a utility payment, or rent/mortgage payment, or payment to any other creditor who reports to a credit bureau.** In other words, they are going to look at everything on your credit report to decide what interest rate you are going to be charged.

While you're working to become financially free, your credit score affects more than just how much interest you'll be charged on debt. It affects insurance premiums, rent charged, utility deposits, and much more. It's important to know where your score comes from and the different ways it can be calculated. The score you're seeing may not be the score your lender is seeing. Why is this, and what can you do about it?

Two major companies are responsible for billions of credit scores provided to lenders and consumers: FICO® and VantageScore® Solutions. The difference between VantageScore vs. FICO credit scores is subtle, reflecting each company's special calculation.

The Fair Isaac Corporation, more commonly known as FICO, scores range from 300 to 850. The higher the number, the better your score. FICO scores are calculated based on how a consumer handles debt and weighted according to the following categories:

- Payment history: 35%
- Amounts owed: 30%
- Length of credit history: 15%
- Credit mix: 10%
- New credit: 10%

FICO scores give the most weight to your payment history and amounts owed. FICO also considers your length of credit history, credit mix, and new credit.

FICO has multiple versions of their credit scoring models, and provides different scoring models to lenders serving different needs. Credit card issuers, auto loan lenders, and mortgage originators may use different FICO scores to make lending decisions.

VantageScores range from 300 to 850, just like FICO scores. However, even though the scores are calculated on the same scale, a VantageScore will be different from a FICO score. VantageScores are based on:

- Payment history: 40%
- Depth of credit: 21%
- Credit utilization: 20%
- Balances: 11%
- Recent credit: 5%
- Available credit: 3%

Since many lenders use FICO Score and consumers often see VantageScores, some lending decisions can take consumers by surprise. The major differences between VantageScores and FICO Score are outlined in the table below. These include the amount of time you have to shop for a loan, the number of categories factored into score calculation, differences in weighted categories, and length of credit history.

	FICO	VantageScore
Shopping Window	45 days	14 days
Categories	5	6
Weighting	Amounts owed weighted more	Payment history weighted more

Some banks and credit card issuers supply VantageScores to their customers for free. Scores are provided largely for consumer education, meaning to help people understand what factors affect their credit score, rather than lending decisions.

Under federal law, everyone is allowed to receive a **free** copy of their credit report once a year from each of the 3 national credit reporting bureaus, TransUnion, Equifax, and Experian. To obtain a free copy of your credit report, go to <u>www.annualcreditreport.com</u>. This is the federal government's **only** officially sanctioned source for obtaining your free reports. This web site shows you how to get your FREE credit report from each bureau. You may apply by telephone or mail. (Consumer alert:

Your FICO scores are not included in your annual free credit report. You will receive solicitations to purchase your FICO score, however, the only source of receiving an accurate FICO score is directly from the three credit reporting agencies or from a lender.)

The first thing you should do is check all of the personal information shown on all 3 credit reports. Make sure they are all accurate. Check all accounts in good standing. Make sure they are all yours. Check all negative accounts. Make sure they are all yours. Then, check all public records. Make sure they are all yours. Finally, examine the list of everyone who has accessed your credit report in the past 2 years. You should have given each of them written permission to access your credit report. If an employer or potential employer has obtained a copy, it should be listed. This is one way you have of verifying whether or not an employer has reviewed your credit report.

We have designed the Credit Report Accuracy Quick Check table to help you quickly determine whether or not everything on your credit report is correct. You should use one for each credit bureau's report.

Credit Report Accuracy Quick Check Experian _____ Equifax _____ TransUnion _____			
	Accurate?		
Section	Yes	No	# Items to Dispute/Correct
Personal Information			
Name			
Social Security Number			
Addresses			
Telephone			
Spouse's First Name			
Employers			
Potentially Negative or Adverse Information			
Public Records			
Credit Items			
Positive Accounts			
Credit Inquiries			

Correcting inaccurate information on your credit report is a very time consuming and frustrating process. It is not unusual for it to take 4 – 6 months to correct items on your credit report. This is the primary reason so many people allow incorrect information to remain on their credit reports. This is also the reason why some people will retain the services of a credit correction firm.

Disputes can be made over the telephone, via the credit bureau's online investigation request file, or through the mail. The credit bureaus prefer disputes submitted via their online program, but it is not necessarily the best way because you do not know if your dispute was received and investigated until you receive a reply. The recommended way of disputing an item on your credit report is via certified mail.

The letters you send will identify all inaccurate items and specifically require the bureaus to verify the information on your report. Information that cannot be verified by the bureaus must be deleted. Incorrect information must be corrected. This allows you to correct the many mistakes appearing on most credit reports.

Prepare a dispute letter. The following is a sample dispute letter.

Date

Your Name
Your Address,
City, State, Zip Code

Complaint Department
Name of Company
Address
City, State, Zip Code

Dear Sir or Madam:
I am writing to dispute the following information in my file. I have circled the items I dispute on the attached copy of the report I received.
This item (identify item(s) disputed by name of source, such as creditors or tax court, and identify type of item, such as credit account, judgment, etc.) is (inaccurate or incomplete) because (describe what is inaccurate or incomplete and why). I am requesting that the item be removed (or request another specific change) to correct the information.
Enclosed are copies of (use this sentence if applicable and describe any enclosed documentation, such as payment records, court documents) supporting my position. Please reinvestigate this (these) matter(s) and (delete or correct) the disputed item(s) as soon as possible.

Sincerely,

Your name

Enclosures: (List what you are enclosing.)

Source: Federal Trade Commission's Consumer Credit Briefcase

Make sure you attach a list of all supporting documentation to prove the validity of your dispute along with a copy of each document. For example, if you are disputing an account reported as in collections even though you paid it in full, you would list the name of the creditor, the item number on the credit report, the account number shown on the credit report, then state why you are disputing the information on the credit report. You must then attach at copy of your receipt for payment and letter from the creditor acknowledging payment in full.

Dispute Letter Attachment			
Creditor	Item #	Acct. #	Dispute and Expected Resolution
XYZ Co.	15	123456	Account paid in full. Change status from open and delinquent to closed, paid in full.

The credit bureaus have 30 days from receipt of your letters to verify the disputed items if your credit report has resulted in adverse action. If you are disputing information received in a "free" credit report, they have 45 days in which to verify any items you are disputing. In some cases, they may request additional time. If you receive a request for more time, review it carefully, and make a copy for your file.

Review the reply from the bureaus. Each credit bureau will, a) verify that the disputed information was correct; b) change the disputed information so that it is correct; c) request more information; or d) remove the item. Each bureau MUST reply in writing. Based upon experience, the bureaus will probably request additional information not only about the item in question, but to verify you are who you say you are.

Review the updated report. Once the credit bureaus have reviewed any requested additional information, each bureau must send a final notice indicating exactly what action they took: whether they verified information, changed items (and exactly how), or removed items. When you get the final report, review it carefully. If it is satisfactory, the process is complete. If not, review it carefully, make a copy for your file, and resend your request for corrections. The more documentation you send to support your claims, the better.

Repeat the process. The credit correction process can be repeated as many times as necessary to correct your report until it is accurate. You may find the same error on more than one credit bureau's report. If you disputed it, one bureau might correct it while another may not. You may want to send a copy of the corrected item from Bureau A to show Bureau B how the item should be reflected.

If all the corrections are made on the first round, it may take 60 days or so. However, usually two or more tries are required to get all the changes made. It is not unusual for the process to take many months.

If deleted items get re-listed on your credit reports, you must be notified prior to a credit bureau re-listing items. Then the item would simply need to be re-challenged. If it was wrong the first time, it will be a simple matter to have it deleted again. If the credit bureau or creditor does not comply, you should contact an attorney to press a civil lawsuit.

HOW TO IMPROVE YOUR CREDIT REPORT

You receive an "inquiry" on your credit report each time a report is requested. In general, credit inquiries can hurt your credit. They can hurt your FICO scores by up to 12 points or more per inquiry, and can remain on credit reports as long as 2 years. While employers do not see your FICO score, they do see credit inquiries. Your credit score is not hurt when a prospective employer pulls your credit. Employers or prospective employers will not see what other employment inquiries have been made.

While there are no guarantees that the suggestions presented in this section will improve your credit report, most people find them helpful. The most important things you can do to improve your credit report are:

- Make sure the report is accurate.
- Pay your bills on time.
- Pay more than the minimum amount due.
- If you have accounts in collection, pay them. If the collection is in dispute, be able to document your position. Paid collection accounts may not improve your credit score, but they do make a difference to employers.
- Do not exceed your credit limit. Ideally keep your balance under half of your credit limit.
- Be honest with yourself, your creditors, and employers when asked about potentially negative items on your credit report.

State laws can impact access rights, fees, notification requirements, and other rights. Experian has links to consumer notification of rights for states which require them.

Not all states require credit bureaus to notify consumers of all their laws regarding consumer credit reports. If you have a question that is not answered, you may want to contact the Consumer Protection Agency for your state.

If your credit score was used to deny you credit or the best loan terms, the lender/creditor to whom you applied must now provide you a copy of your credit score upon which they based their decision.

WEEK 21
CONSUMER PROTECTION LAWS YOU NEED TO KNOW

"Nothing makes God more supreme and more central in worship than when a people are utterly persuaded that nothing - not money or prestige or leisure or family or job or health or sports or toys or friends - nothing is going to bring satisfaction to their sinful, guilty, aching hearts besides God." —John Piper

---

Do you know what your rights are if you fall behind on paying a debt? Do you know what your privacy rights are? We've talked about your consumer credit reports, but did you know that you have the right to see what insurance companies, healthcare providers, and financial institutions say about you? Consumer protection laws exit because what you don't know can hurt you. You and only you are responsible for the accuracy of consumer reports. You and only you are responsible for learning what rights you have to protect yourself and your family from harassing debt collectors, unwanted telephone calls, etc.

FAIR AND ACCURATE CREDIT TRANSACTIONS ACT OF 2003 (FACTA)

You have a right to a **free** credit report from each of the major credit reporting bureaus (Experian, Equifax, & TransUnion) every week! www.annualcreditreport.com

FAIR AND ACCURATE CREDIT TRANSACTIONS ACT OF 2003 (FACTA)

You have a right to a **free** credit report from a fourth credit reporting bureau, Core Logic, once every 12 months.
www.corelogic.com
1-877-532-8778

FAIR AND ACCURATE CREDIT TRANSACTIONS ACT OF 2003 (FACTA)

You have a right to a **free** specialty consumer report from Medical Information Bureau (MIB) once every 12 months.
http://www.mib.com/html/request_your_record.html
1-866-692-6901

FAIR AND ACCURATE CREDIT TRANSACTIONS ACT OF 2003 (FACTA)

You have a right to a **free** specialty consumer report from each of the major insurance consumer reporting bureaus (LexisNexis and Insurance Service Office) once every 12 months.
https://personalreports.lexisnexis.com/index.jsp
1-866-312-8076
www.iso.com/offices_contacts/index.html
1-800-627-3487

FAIR AND ACCURATE CREDIT TRANSACTIONS ACT OF 2003 (FACTA)

You have a right to a **free** specialty consumer report from Chex Systems and check writing history reports once every 12 months.
ChexSystems https://www.consumerdebit.com/consumerinfo/us/en/freereport.htm
1-800-428-9623

Shared Check Authorization Network (SCAN)
www.consumerdebit.com/consumerinfo/us/en/consumerreports/index.htm#TopOfPage
1-800-262-7771

TeleCheck www.telecheck.com
1-800-835-3243

FAIR AND ACCURATE CREDIT TRANSACTIONS ACT OF 2003 (FACTA)

You have a right to a **free** residential tenant reports once every 12 months. Many firms create these reports. The most common ones are LexisNexis Resident History Report, CoreLogic SafeRent, Tenant Data, and RentBureau.

LexisNexis
https://personalreports.lexisnexis.com/resident_history_report.jsp
1-877-448-5732

CoreLogic
http://corelogic.saferent.com/consumer_relations/forms/index.php
1-888-333-2413

Tenant Data
www.tenantdata.com/downloads.php
1-800-228-1837

RentBureau
www.experian.com/rentbureau/rental-payment.html
1-877-704-4519

FAIR AND ACCURATE CREDIT TRANSACTIONS ACT OF 2003 (FACTA)

You have a right to a **free** employment report once every 12 months from The Work Number, LexisNexis, and Social Intelligence Corp. If employment is denied based upon background checks, you have the right to a FREE copy of the report provided the prospective employer.

The Work Number
www.theworknumber.com
1-800-996-7566

LexisNexis
https://personalreports.lexisnexis.com/employment_history_report.jsp
1-866-312-8075

Social Intelligence Corp
http://socialmediatoday.com/steve-olenski/309371/why-number-seven-just-got-unlucky-social-media-users

FAIR AND ACCURATE CREDIT TRANSACTIONS ACT OF 2003 (FACTA)

You have the **right** to Opt-Out for Marketing. This means you can stop a corporation from sharing information about you with their affiliates.

For more on the existing opt-outs, see PRC Fact Sheet 24, Protecting Financial Privacy in the New Millennium: The Burden Is on You, www.privacyrights.org/fs/fs24-finpriv.htm, and Fact 24a, Financial Privacy: How to Read Your Opt-Out Notices, www.privacyrights.org/fs/fs24a-optout.htm.

FAIR AND ACCURATE CREDIT TRANSACTIONS ACT OF 2003 (FACTA)

You must receive a notice if you are offered credit on terms "materially" less favorable than the terms others received from the creditor.

This covers the situation where you apply for a loan and, although you get the loan, you have to pay a higher interest rate than most people because of something in your credit history. If this happens, you are entitled to notice plus a free copy of your credit report. Like many other provisions included in FACTA, the risk-based pricing notices aim to give consumers the tools to identify and an opportunity to correct inaccuracies in their credit reports.

The risk-based pricing notice requirement does not override the notice requirement consumer reporting agencies are required to make to "users" of consumer reports. www.ftc.gov.

DODD FRANK WALL STREET REFORM & CONSUMER PROTECTION ACT OF 2010 (DODD FRANK)

You have the right to have all costs, i.e. fees, risks, and conflicts of interest clearly and concisely stated.

Subtitle A – Increasing Investor Protection
401K providers must communicate this information on each participant's statement.

DODD FRANK WALL STREET REFORM & CONSUMER PROTECTION ACT OF 2010 (DODD FRANK)

The SEC has the authority to impose a standard of care and define the fiduciary duty between broker-dealers and investment advisors and their customers.

Subtitle A – Increasing Investor Protection

This provision is currently being challenged by broker-dealers.

DODD FRANK WALL STREET REFORM & CONSUMER PROTECTION ACT OF 2010 (DODD FRANK)

You have the right to choose whether or not you pay overdraft fees. See your bank or credit union for specific details.

DODD FRANK WALL STREET REFORM & CONSUMER PROTECTION ACT OF 2010 (DODD FRANK)

You have the right to receive your credit scores **free of charge** if you are refused credit or charged a higher price for credit than most consumers because of your score.

This provision is an acceptable alternative to the risk based pricing section of The Fair and Accurate Credit Transactions Act of 2003 (FACTA).

FAIR DEBT COLLECTION PRACTICES ACT

You have the right to require a debt collector send you written proof that you are the legal debtor for the debt they are attempting to collect.

FAIR DEBT COLLECTION PRACTICES ACT

Creditors and debt collectors have a limited time in which to sue you for unpaid debts. The Statute of Limitation in the State of Texas is 4 years.

However, any time you make a payment on a debt, regardless of the

amount of the payment, the clock is reset and the 4 year count starts over. Acknowledging a debt as yours will also reset the clock.
Statute of Limitation and Time Barred Debt, www.ftc.gov

TELEPHONE CONSUMER PROTECTION ACT OF 1991

You have the right to put both your home phone and cell phones on the National Do Not Call Registry **free** of charge.

Scammers have been making phone calls claiming to represent the National Do Not Call Registry. The calls claim to provide an opportunity to sign up for the Registry. These calls are not coming from the Registry or the Federal Trade Commission, and you should not respond to these calls. To add your number to the Registry you can call 888-382-1222 from the phone you wish to register, or go to www.donotcall.gov.

Your registration will not expire. Telephone numbers placed on the National Do Not Call Registry will remain on it permanently due to the Do-Not-Call Improvement Act of 2007, which became law in February 2008.

HOW TO RECOGNIZE AND PROTECT YOURSELF FROM SCAMS

"A political race today, even a primary, is $150 million. The whole political system has become obscene in terms of the absurd amount of money that is required to compete. Just put it on ESPN and call it a sporting event." —Mike Huckabee

---

"Your vehicle's warranty has expired! Act now before it's too late!" Sometimes this message comes in the mail as a postcard. Sometimes it is in a sealed envelope. Sometimes you might receive a telephone call. Whatever the delivery method, it is most probably from someone trying to get you to send them money in exchange for ______ . That's right, nothing.

Every year literally billions of dollars are stolen from individuals just like you and me. The following are just a few of the scams currently seeking your hard-earned money:

- Disaster relief
- War refugee relief

- Business opportunities – especially multi-level marketing or other which costs you a lot of money
- Online surveys, games, giveaways where purchase or registration fee is required
- Subscription services with no clear or easy cancellation option
- Online or mail order pharmaceuticals and healthcare supplies
- International lotteries
- Business services, i.e. auto and home warranties
- Investments
- Government impersonators, i.e. tax collector
- Animal relief

And more. Unfortunately, many more.

Scams have become so sophisticated these days it's easy to be caught off guard. I recently received a phone call with the name of my city on the caller ID. Because I live in a small town where I actually know people who work for the city, the mayor, and several city council members, I didn't think anything of answering the call. It turned out to be a scam call. I received another phone call where the caller ID read CVS. Again, I answered it thinking it might be about my father's prescription. Nope. It was another scam call.

The National Do Not Call Registry, www.donotcall.gov, DOES NOT block calls from scammers who ignore the registry. This registry was created to stop unwanted sales calls from legitimate telemarketers. It does not apply to political groups, survey takers, charitable organizations, debt collectors, or informational calls. There is a major caveat to which you need to be alert: If you have done business with a company or have given "written permission" to a company, they can legally make sales calls to you even if you have registered your phone number. Most of the time, "written permission" is buried in fine print as part of a website's terms and conditions, or as part of a receipt. Some companies have structured the language in such a way that if you don't "accept", you can't do business with them.

Robocalls, a call that plays a recorded message, are illegal unless you have given the company "written permission" to contact you. However, recent technological advancements in artificial intelligence (AI) have the Federal Trade Commission (FTC) and other consumer watch-dogs issuing a plethora of scam alerts. Many scammers are using tools like ChatGPT to try to scam people out of their money. Scammers use AI voice-generating software to mimic the voice of someone you know. They will call and use the fake voice to try and convince you to send money to cover some sort of emergency. One of the reasons this scam is so convincing is because fraudsters have started using AI chatbots to create real-time responses.

In the past, telephone scams were usually pre-recorded messages. Most of the time, the pre-recorded responses didn't make sense in the conversation. These days, scammers are using sophisticated technology to generate surprisingly realistic scripts with adaptive real-time responses. This makes it much more difficult to determine if you're speaking to a robot — or someone you really know.

Experts say the best way to avoid telephone-based scams is to not answer the phone unless you know who the caller is, but using the two experiences I had, even when you think you know who is calling you, it may be someone else. This "imposter phone scam" is the most common occurrence of fraud resulting in millions of dollars stolen every year. When in doubt, tell the person you will call them back, hang up, and then call the number you have for that contact.

One of the saddest scams are "Romance" or "Lonely Hearts" scams. These are usually perpetrated against middle-age and senior widows. They can start in person or online. The widow – or widower – is flattered by the attention they are receiving by the fraudster. They look forward to the interaction from this person who fills their lonely hours. The person becomes a financial leach sucking up as much of the widow(er)'s money as possible. Sometimes it's hard cash, but usually it begins with "gifts", clothing, meals, and vacations. Then comes the hard luck story. The scammer needs to go take care of some emergency, but doesn't have the wherewithal to get there. Lonely Heart buys the airplane ticket. Scammer calls regularly with updates, each of which is going to require more time away and more money. Lonely Heart sends more money and the cycle continues until someone finally intervenes and convinces Lonely Heart to stop sending money. By then Lonely Heart is out thousands of dollars.

During the years I counseled individuals filing for bankruptcy protection, the saddest were the sessions with Mr. or Mrs. Lonely Heart. Sometimes a family member was the one who intervened, but usually it was a debt collector.

Scammers will try to get you to order healthcare items which "cost you nothing"! Items range from Covid-19 test kits, to back and knee braces, to insulin products. They will tell you the items are covered by your insurance company, and for your convenience, the scammer will collect from your insurance "on your behalf." Medicare and Medicaid recipients are the most frequent targets of these scams. The typical telephone scam tends to go like this:

"Hello, Mrs. Consumer? This is Wendi calling from Acme Medical Supply. I'm calling to make sure you received the Covid-19 test kits we sent you."

You, Mrs. Consumer may or may not have received unsolicited Covid-19 test kits, so you respond, "I didn't request a Covid-19 test kit."

The scammer then says, "Well your doctor wants to make sure you stay as healthy as possible. These are provided a not cost to you by your insurance company, which is Medicare, correct?"

And the scam goes from there. Most healthcare product scammers obtained your personal information from hacked medical databases, although some actually purchase lists of Medicare and Medicaid recipients. Medicare is aware of these scams and would like consumers to report them more frequently than they currently are.

How do you protect yourself and those you love from falling prey to a scam? Some of the following tips can be found at www.ftc.gov:

- In the wake of a natural disaster or another crisis, give to established charities rather than a new one

- Don't respond to any message requesting your personal or financial information
- Only install apps or software from trusted sources
- Read your bills and monthly statements regularly whether on paper or online
- Wiring money is like sending cash: once it's gone, you can't get it back
- Don't send money to someone you don't know
- Don't agree to deposit a check from you don't know and then wire money back to them
- If someone calls you from a company and asks for payment over the telephone, don't give them any information. If you want to make a payment over the telephone, hang up and call the company to whom you want to make a payment.
- Don't play a foreign lottery
- Remember there is no such thing as a sure thing
- Talk to your healthcare provider before buying health products or signing up for medical treatments
- Know where an offer comes from and who you're dealing with
- Beware of false urgency. Don't let anyone pressure you into giving them any information about yourself.

When in doubt, just say "NO."

LIFTING OTHERS

"Seek not greater wealth, but simpler pleasure; not higher fortune, but deeper felicity. The rich cannot accumulate wealth without the co-operation of the poor in society. A man's true wealth hereafter is the good he has done to his fellowmen." —Mahatma Gandhi

---

By now you should be well on your way to financial freedom. You're returning unto God a portion of that with which He has blessed you. You've learned some of the methods used to entice you to spend more than you planned. You're preparing every needful thing for turbulent times which befall everyone some time in their lives. You're recognizing and controlling spending which doesn't help you reach your goals and priorities. This means you've learned to say "NO!" Because you're smarter with your money, you're a better steward. A good steward, like the good shepherd, gently lifts those who need a hand over the rocky terrain. As you lift others, He will lift you.

You may feel as though you are at the end of hard-fought battle. The truth is that there are many more battles to win before the war is over. Like the Good Shepherd, you must remain ever vigilant to the temptations you will encounter during life's journey. Teaching your children, extended family, friends, and associates the joy which comes from being financially free is an ongoing process.

Celebrate each small accomplishment in creative ways which can be shared with others. For example, every time you pay off a creditor, plant a "debt free" tree, bush, or native plant. Invite family, friends, and neighbors to your planting ceremony. Explain that as the plant takes root, it not only helps the ecosystem, but serves as a reminder of what you accomplished. You might be able to obtain a free tree or other plant from your local agricultural society or university. One place to try is the National Wildlife Foundation, https://www.nwf.org/Trees-for-Wildlife/Request-Trees.

Another example is to host a balloon party. Cut up your final bill or note into tiny pieces. Put a piece of the bill into a balloon before blowing it up. As colorful balloons are released into the air, you wave good-bye to the noose that used to be around your neck. If it's a vehicle you paid off, drive through town with a banner on the vehicle proclaiming no more payments! Have fun accepting kudos from strangers while encouraging them at the same time.

Sometimes it's easier to see someone else's problems than our own. Often, we are so caught up in our own daily minutia we don't recognize how much progress we have made. We tend to be our own worst enemy. We are over critical and fail to recognize – and verbally applaud – the simple, small steps being made towards financial freedom. Everyone needs encouragement regardless of age and regardless of how far along the continuum they are in their quest to be financially free. Organize a support network.

It doesn't matter whether you form a formal group which meets on a regular basis, or you have a coach or friend to whom you can turn when you get discouraged or tempted. One former client organized a monthly pot luck where everyone brought a budget-friendly dish, (and recipe), to share. (Some of these recipes are included in the *Financially Free in 23 Weeks Workbook.*) In order to learn which dishes her picky-eater family would enjoy, she made them taste each dish then vote on the "dish of the month." The winning dish received a Picky-Eater certificate.

You might choose to start your own company as a *Financially Free in 23 Weeks* licensee. The important thing is to have, and actively participate in, a support system. As a contributing member, you will find that as you listen to and provide encouragement to others, you will lift them. Don't forget to include God in your support system. He will never fail you.

It is often helpful to see how others resolve – or don't resolve – financial challenges. In addition to sacred writings, personal financial management issues have been addressed in both classical and contemporary literature. Shakespeare wrote,

---

"Neither a borrower nor a lender be;
    For loan oft loses both itself and friend,
    And borrowing dulls the edge of husbandry."

HAMLET ACT 1, SCENE III, LINE 75-77

In *David Copperfield*, Charles Dickens penned, "Annual income twenty pounds, annual expenditure nineteen and six, result happiness. Annual income twenty pounds, annual expenditure twenty pounds ought and six, result misery." (Ch. 12)

I have worked with churches, universities, and public libraries which wanted to offer eclectic programs to their communities. We put together programs whereby we examined the age-old conundrum of debt. The most popular turned out to be book discussion groups which pulled from the following suggested reading list:

- **Confessions of a Shopaholic** by Sophie Kinsella
- **David Copperfield** by Charles Dickens
- **Death on the Installment Plan** by Louis-Ferdinand Céline
- **Financial Peace** by Dave Ramsey
- **Financially Every After: The Couples' Guide to Managing Money** by Jeff D. Opdyke

- **Germinal** by Émile Zola
- **Hamlet** by William Shakespeare
- **Madame Bovary** by Gustave Flaubert
- **MoneyZen** by Manisha Thakor
- **Pride and Prejudice** by Jane Austen
- **Rich Dad, Poor Dad** by Robert Kiyosaki
- **So Much for That** by Lionel Shriver
- **The Girl With The Dragon Tattoo** by Stieg Larsson
- **The Giving Tree** by Shel Silverstein
- **The Good Earth** by Pearl S. Buck
- **The Testament** by John Grisham
- **The Total Money Makeover** by Dave Ramsey
- **The Ultimate Gift** by Jim Stovall
- **The Women** by T.C. Boyle
- **Vanity Fair** by William Makepeace Thackeray

Members of the group were asked to identify similarities between themselves and the characters in the book. What motivated the characters to act as they did? How did their actions affect others? What value did the characters place on money – earning, spending, and saving? How did the characters view others with money? How did the characters view others without money? Can money buy happiness? Etc. There was a core group of members each month, but there were also new members each month adding unique insights and perspectives. The concluding question each month was, "What, if anything, did you learn about personal financial management that you want to apply to your own life?"

I walked away from each book discussion uplifted. I was supposed to be the facilitator, yet I never ceased to stand in awe of the fellowship which developed each month as participants lifted each other up. Being financially free is not a one and done event. It is a lifelong mindset. In the *Financially Free in 23 Weeks Workbook*, you will find three of the outlines I used for discussions. Use them to provide yourself with new perspectives. Have some fun with them. Use them to lift others.

ABOUT THE AUTHOR

Elizabeth Hubbard has more than 20 years' experience providing budgeting and personal financial education and counseling to thousands throughout the country. She has developed in person and virtual financial literacy programs for the U.S. Department of Justice's Executive Office of the U.S. Trustee, the U.S. Department of Labor, the State of Texas Department of Assistive and Rehabilitative Services, U.S. Army Reserves Family Readiness program, Texas Workforce Services, and other public and private entities.

Elizabeth co-authored *Fight On!: World War II and Cold War Experiences of Lt. Commander John R. "Jack" Hubbard, USNR*, and wrote the Foreword to *Purple Mountains & Wilderness: True Stories of the Great American West*, both of which are Amazon bestsellers. She has edited multiple other award-winning books. She has also written or co-authored peer-reviewed academic journal articles, white papers, and technical manuals.

Elizabeth holds an MBA from Pepperdine University and a BA from Brigham Young University – Hawaii.

9 781735 833873